THE BLESSED DAYS AND NIGHTS OF THE
ISLAMIC YEAR

The Blessed Days and Nights of the
ISLAMIC YEAR

Hüseyin Algül

Translated by Jane L. Kandur

Light

New Jersey
2005

Published by The Light, Inc.
26 Worlds Fair Dr. Suite C
Somerset, New Jersey, 08873, USA

www.thelightpublishing.com

Translated from Turkish by Jane L. Kandur

Library of Congress Cataloging-in-Publication Data

Algül, Hüseyin.
   [Mübarek gün ve geceler. English]
   The blessed days and nights of the Islamic year / Hüseyin Algül.
       p. cm.
   Includes bibliographical references.
   ISBN 1-932099-93-X
   1. Fasts and feasts--Islam. 2. Islam--Customs and practices. 3. Religious life-
-Islam. 4. Calendar, Islamic. I. Title.
BP186.A5813 2005
297.3'6--dc22

                                        2005024660

Printed by
Çağlayan A.Ş., Izmir - Turkey
September 2005

TABLE OF CONTENTS

INTRODUCTION

God chose Ramadan from amongst all the months; He chose the Night of Qadr (Power) from all the nights; from all the places in the world, He chose Makka; from all the people, He chose Prophet Muhammad, peace and blessings be upon him; and from all the days, He chose Friday. In the same vein, according to a hadith (the Prophet's sayings, or traditions), believers who pray in the Masjid al-Haram, the Masjid al-Nabi, or the Masjid al-Aqsa are bestowed with more blessings than if they had prayed in any other mosque.

Islamic sources tell us that of the lunar months[1] Rajab, Shaban, and Ramadan are more blessed than other months and that of these months, the nights of Raghaib, the Miraj, Bara'a, and Qadr are significant. Fasting for six days during the lunar month of Shawwal, during the days of Ashura in Muharram, on the night of the Mawlid, which is generally accepted as falling on the twelfth of Rabi al-Awwal, and during the first ten days of Dhu al-Hijja are all considered to be blessed actions. The nights and days of the Eids (festivals) are very important, as is fasting on Mondays and Thursdays, and of course, Friday. However, it is highly probable that over the centuries some unfounded traditions have become intermingled with what is actually true. For this reason, we find ourselves in a position where there is a need to bring to the fore correct knowledge concerning these beliefs. Every Muslim should make an effort to learn what is correct concerning the holy days and nights. In this way, they will engage in the prayers, penitence, repentance, self-accounting, chanting of remembrance, and congratulating one another in a more conscious way.

As this book is intended to be only a small booklet, notes with regard to the sources have been added at the end. As well as using the primary sources of Kutub al-Sitta (the six reliable books of hadith compilation) some other sources, like *al-Taj* and *Riyadh al-Salihin* (The Garden of the Righteous), which were compiled from the former, have also been used; it is usually easier for the general reader to have access to the latter two. Sources that have been used more than once have not been repeated. A bibliography of some of the sources from which we have benefited is listed at the end of the book. We hope that the book will serve as a useful reference for new Muslims. Although the style adopted may sound as if it is addressing a Muslim audience, we believe the presentation also provides easy access to useful information for those who want to find out more about Islamic tradition. One final issue to keep in mind is that there are differences in the way the blessed days and nights are celebrated throughout the Islamic world due to the cultural and historical developments of different nations. We have done our best to avoid culture-specific content and to relate all information to authentic sources.

I would like to thank Kathleen St.Onge for her invaluable comments on the style and content of this book.

Hüseyin Algül
Bursa 2004

THE BLESSED DAYS AND NIGHTS
IN MUSLIM SOCIETY

The life of a person never goes in a straight line; it consists of hills and valleys. Happiness is wrapped up in sadness. Many times we can be just as happy as we are sad, or as sad as we are happy. This may change from time to time. Just as happy events make people happy, problems and stress can also shake them, causing them to come face to face with indelible pain. It is almost impossible to outline the life of a person from birth to death in one straight line; if every person were to examine the path of their own life, they would notice that it is surrounded by steep hills, dips, valleys, and inclines. These are symbols of the obstacles that lay along the path of our life.

So what is one to do? A person should be grateful when they are content, patient when they face difficulties; they must deal with problems in a clear-headed manner, taking precautions and working in a systematic way to find solutions. In short, one must be grateful, patient, and persevering. Gratitude will increase the rewards God sends to us, and patience will help us overcome our troubles. Moreover, gratitude and patience bring their own rewards.

In accordance with this, a Muslim society regards the blessed days and nights as an important opportunity to increase their gratitude when happy and their patience when in trouble. Imagine; you are on a long journey, the day is hot, you are exhausted, sweat is dripping from your brow, your mouth is dry, your legs are shaky. You would give anything for a glass of cold water, for a shady spot in which to rest. You shade your eyes with your hand and peer to the horizon . . . what is that you see? A garden with flowing water, singing birds, and cool shade. Naturally, you want to go sit there, cool off and rest. After a rest you take up your journey with a renewed hope.

For Muslims, this resting place is the blessed days and nights; they are a way-station or a favorite haunt in which a person can rest, catch their breath, and prepare for the rest of the journey, taking an overview of their life and analyzing deeds and thoughts (*muhasaba*[2]) between the tiring worrying trials of everyday life. When Muslims take stock of their life, they need to ask themselves, how is it possible to increase the good deeds, the useful and kind acts that they have performed? How can they eliminate their mistakes and faults? Muslims try to find the answers to these questions within themselves. They repent for any sins they have committed. It is at this time that Muslims resolve to eliminate any shortcomings in their worship. They read the Qur'an, they eliminate any faults or deficiencies in their religious knowledge, they look through books and magazines for information that can illuminate their knowledge, correct it, and develop it. They listen to sermons and lectures on these subjects, particularly to those concerning the Qur'an and the Sunna (the Prophet's examples), and they contemplate the messages that they have been given, learning from these lessons. From all of these, Muslims are able to attain the principles that enlighten their heart, and they throw themselves into new efforts to implement the religion in their lives once again.

At the same time, the days and nights of Ramadan, the Night of Qadr, Friday and Friday night, can all be a means for forgiveness. The joyful awareness of this fact acts as a very powerful spiritual cure. Muslims are able to consult with this spiritual healer free of charge.

Let's examine this matter a bit closer; if one of your internal organs were to cause you great pain, making you writhe in agony, would you not immediately run to consult your doctor? Of course you would. You go to the doctor, receive treatment, and relieved of pain, return home. You are now cured; you are eased of your pain. You sigh with relief; life will go on. We thank the doctor for restoring us to health; we thank God Almighty.

We are willing to take the medicine prescribed by our doctor when we experience any physical discomfort; likewise we should go to some effort to extricate ourselves from the sins that darken our world, strangle our souls, and grieve our hearts. So let us consider what we can do in such a situation. In Islamic literature, the effort to cleanse oneself of sins is called repentance (*tawba*) or penitence (*istighfar*). There are certain periods of time that allow people to increase and focus on repentance, not only vocally, but also with their hearts. There is no question that one can repent of one's sins at any time, but the days listed above are periods that ease the ability to focus on repentance and to repent with the entire soul. The blessed days and nights are periods that allow Muslims to direct their inner selves toward repentance. These periods are important opportunities for Muslims to take a significant step in the direction of eliminating these sins and progressing toward goodness and beauty. On these days and nights, with no intermediary, a person delves into their inner world, remaining alone with Almighty God. They pray to Him, repent and make penance, striving to recapture the inner peace that has been shattered by their sins. In this way, the holy days and nights are like a spiritual doctor who heals the soul with his special spiritual prescriptions.

One of the things that Muslims must examine on the blessed days and nights is their relationships with their neighbors, work colleagues, and business partners. One shares the same community with them; one may even adopt the same ideas. But in some matters, in some details, perceptions and comprehensions may differ. The cause of some of these differences in a few matters may be caused by temperament. Is it possible to accept these differences without sacrificing peace of mind? Is it possible to be an exemplary person in the community? Is it possible to combine correct actions with correct services, despite these differences? Does one provide neighbors, customers, or those to whom services are given, with a sense of security? Is one a tolerant person, some-one who can be trusted, who is good-humored, who can estab-lish good relationships, who greets others, who replies greetings, a person who treats children with tenderness and adults with respect, who smiles and speaks kindly, a person who can deal with diffi-cult situations?

Muslims try to answer these questions on the blessed days and nights; they evaluate their actions in their social life, and they have the chance to renew or change their behavior. From time to time, human beings undergo a process of change; in such a situation, it is important to ensure that the direction this change takes is toward what is positive, beneficial, or appropri-ate. In this way, the blessed days and nights open a door toward positive change, enabling one to overcome life's obstacles more easily and to gain easier access to the road to success.

Even if Muslims try to fulfill the duties of worship most of the time, they may find us in a position where they have neg-lected to engage in the good actions that arise from developing social relationships with the people around them. Consequently, their belief and worship will not suffuse into other areas, nor will they be manifested in their daily life. But Islam is complete; it covers every aspect of life . . . A Muslim's belief necessitates servitude. Worship includes the environment and everyday life, as well as other forms of worship, like prayer, fasting, paying alms, pilgrimage, and sacrifice; worship makes a whole. If a conscious sense of responsibility is taken, if worship is put into the daily life, providing beneficial services and work that is of use, then one possesses the blessings of not only worship, but also of servi-tude, human perfection, and maturity.

If one can take stock of belief and worship in their daily lives on these blessed days and nights, it is without a doubt that they have taken an important step on the way to being one of God's sincere servants. If Muslims can succeed in this, they will be better able to understand that it is necessary to give as much importance to faith as it is to give to worship, and to give as much importance to one's deeds as to worship, and they will be able to see that they will be greatly blessed if they treat their neighbors well, are honest in business transactions, give importance to quality in their products, and help the poor and estranged to the same degree that they believe and worship.

At the same time, each blessed day and night is an opportunity to take stock of one's relationships with one's children and relatives. In today's world, it is quite commonplace that relationships between mothers, fathers, children and other relatives are problematical. When we talk to the people around us and share our troubles, it is easy to see that nearly everyone says the same thing. Everyone takes a deep breath, and tells us with heartfelt sorrow how their children are not concerned enough with important matters, how they do not share their joys and sorrows. The blessed days and nights have been given as an opportunity to come together with children of all ages, grandchildren, relatives and friends, in order to celebrate together and to pray together. This is something that should be taken advantage of.

When the blessed days and nights are looked at from another aspect, it is the folklore-culture that attracts our attention. The fast-breaking meals bring together friends and less fortunate people, whereas *tarawih* (the special congregational prayer held after breaking the fast) is an occasion for developing new forms of companionships. Generally, during Ramadan, friends of an age gather and go to a different mosque every night in an atmosphere of joy and celebration. The discussions after the *tarawih*, and the offers of sweets and tea, carry on until the small hours. Sometimes, these discussion circles are enhanced by Sufi music. After the performance of the *tarawih* prayer, these discussions provide one with a spiritual joy, instilling peace into one's heart on the road home. These discussions and acts of hospitality take place in teahouses, meeting houses, or homes that are located near the mosque. The Night of Power is celebrated all across the Muslim world with a special commitment to prayer. Families visit different mosques and strive to maintain their vigil until morning in order to benefit from the blessings promised for this night.

For Muslim children, Ramadan and the festivities, in particular, have a very special meaning. Waking up very early in the morning for the predawn meal is exciting for them—in many homes, to the song of the drummer—although it is not very easy to do throughout the month. The excitement and flurry of trying to find a place in or outside the mosque for the Eid prayer is also unforgettable. Everyone exchanges good wishes with neighbors and friends right outside the mosque, on the street, and then the festival traditions continue with sweets and lovely food being offered in homes. Friends discuss how the sweets have turned out this year; recipes are swapped for future Eids, and the celebration starts, taking in a wide area of acquaintances from neighbors, close relatives and colleagues, business partners, distant relatives, friends and acquaintances. During this time, even though the way of celebration may differ from village to village, town to town, city to city, or country to country, the idea is the same: to congratulate, bless, pray, and to express good wishes for the future.

AN EID DAY IN A TURKISH VILLAGE

Having broached this subject, I would like to share the cultural and folk history of the villages in Turkey with the readers of today. When we were children, we would wait in great anticipation for Eid. If you wonder why this was, the answer is simple: our families prepared special outfits for us to wear on that day. We would get up early on the morning of the Eid, put on our spanking new outfits, and take the thin skewers that we had prepared the day before from willow or popular branches, and set out on a tour the neighborhood. We would skewer the gifts that the neighbors gave us; some would give sweets, some money, while others would offer us deep-fried buns. We would return home with an overloaded skewer and bind the two ends together to form a ring. Of course, we were soon out on the street again, offering our excess to the other children in the neighborhood. In this way, children acted as a means to ensure that every household had offered something to every neighbor. After the Eid prayer, every house would put the food that had been prepared for the feast on a copper tray, which, without much time being lost, would be taken to the *köy odası* (village hall). Four banquets would be prepared, one for the elderly, one for the grownups, one for the young people and one for the children. The grownups, assisted by able youths, would serve the groups in order, starting from the elders. In this way, the Eid feast was consumed with a festive air. Then the copper trays would be taken home and the hall would be prepared for visitors from other areas. Tea, coffee, and sherbet were prepared. A group of young people would stay to serve the elders and leaders of the neighborhood, as well as important visitors, while the others would go to the other halls in the village and visit the locals there. In this way, the whole village would be able to celebrate the Eid together. But the visiting at Eid did not finish here. Particularly on days when the weather was good, everyone would gather and go to the cemetery together; first they would pray *Zuhr* (noon) prayer as a congregation, and then after the prayers, the imam would read both Ya Sin (Chapter 36) and Mulk (Chapter 67), or one of these, sending the prayers to the souls of the dead. Then, en masse, the graves of loved ones would be visited. Thus, not only were the living visited on Eid, the dead were also remembered.

I have pondered this my whole life; the visiting of graves, one after the other, on Eid mornings taught me that death was a part of life. Every Eid, I felt as if I were meeting and talking with the souls of ancestors who lay under the cypress and almond trees.

After the visit to the cemetery, at dusk, the children would untie their skewers, and everyone—children, parents, young and old—would gather to eat supper together. In this way, a truly blessed meal was prepared. Later, if the time of year permitted, sports activities like wrestling matches started with, of course, the children going first. The champions would be presented with a trophy.

These are all reflections of the culture and folk tradition that could be seen on such days and nights. These gatherings strengthened understanding, agreement, and cooperation within the community. Those who had fallen out would make up. Social life was fortified, common traditions and sharing were increased, and communal feelings developed. The idea of a community as a "bringer together" was seen in actuality on the holy days and nights. People found positive meanings behind the reality of what we call "communal conscience," and national awareness developed and increased at these times.

THE WEEK OF THE HOLY BIRTH

The oldest name for the holy birth of Prophet Muhammad in history is *Mawlid al-Nabi* (literally "the birth of the Prophet"). The ceremonies, activities, and celebrations of the Holy Birth arose out of love for our Prophet. These activities have intensified, until they have all come together in the celebrations of the anniversary of Prophet Muhammad's birth.

At this point, we come across an individual who holds a significant place in Turkish Muslim history: Muzaffer al-Din Gokbori. A senior officer in the Seljuk State, Muzaffer al-Din Gokbori (1154-1232) was in charge of Arbil, located in what is now northern Iraq. He was also the brother-in-law of Salah al-Din, the sultan of the Ayyubi State.

Gokbori was a very sincere Muslim and a great lover of Prophet Muhammad. He established a variety of charitable institutions in his time. Strangers and foreigners could stay in safety and comfort at the guesthouses he established. He built hospitals for the ill, rest homes for widows, and orphanages for children. He hired wet-nurses for babies whose mothers had died. He prepared special institutions to take care of the crippled and blind. He also established an institution to hand out provisions to the needy. He opened middle-level and higher schools for students, and he appointed able teachers to these institutions. He gave great importance to competitions in knowledge, scientific debate, and lectures. Many times he would join in these scientific-cultural activities as a listener. He set up a special team to ensure the security of those who were passing through the territory on their way to Hajj. He would send presents and aid to the needy in Makka and Madina.

Gokbori would bring such activities to the highest level at the Mawlid al-Nabi. Gokbori would organize festivities, visit the ill, treat them for free, and help the poor and needy in the week following the anniversary of the birth of Prophet Muhammad. During this week, special festivities were organized for children. Scholars, poets, and those who served the community were all remembered, and people who had benefited society were brought to the fore and awarded prizes. Throughout the week, scholars would enlighten the people on the life of Prophet Muhammad and provided them with information concerning the Qur'an and Islam.

Because of these activities, children, young people, the elderly, the healthy, the sick, the handicapped, merchants, tradesmen, students, teachers, scholars, local politicians, people who served the religion, soldiers, and bureaucrats—in short, people from every occupation and every age group—would be brought together because of their love for the Prophet, and they would be happy and at peace in their union. These activities brought the people and the state together in cooperation and unity at the highest level.

The Turkish experience of Mawlid al-Nabi continued during the Ottoman period. The Mawlid Parade signified the most prominent among all other activities dedicated to celebrate the Prophet's Birth. On the anniversary of the birth of the Prophet, the Sheikhulislam (the highest religious authority), the viziers, other high-level bureaucrats, famous scholars, well-known preachers, the people, and the Sultan would gather in Sultanahmet Mosque in Istanbul. After the arrival of the Sultan, sermons and speeches would be delivered. Later the famous poem of *Wasilat al-Najat*, or as it was popularly known, the *Mawlid*, by Suleyman Çelebi, would be read, and the congregation would be offered dates that had come from Madina.

The birth of the Prophet is celebrated in some Muslim countries with different activities. In recent years, an official program, "The Week of the Holy Birth" has been held in Turkey around the time that marks the anniversary of the Prophet's birth. Islamic scholars, in cooperation with students and local religious leaders, organize a variety of programs for one week in every part of the country; these programs are concerned with the Prophet, Islam, and the Qur'an. In these programs, people from every age and walk of life come together because of their love for the Prophet. Thus, Islam is explained to masses of people illuminated by knowledge. This joyful gathering and sincere sharing of emotions increases cooperation among people; this, in turn, plays an important role in unity and cooperation.

Yes...this fountain of deep attachment and respect for the Prophet should continue to play joyfully. The love for God and the Prophet is the source of all love.

God Almighty did not create people to fight; rather He created them to serve, love, and benefit one another. So come, let us keep this river of love flowing fast and let us bring this service to humanity, God's vicegerents on Earth, without any expectation of reward.

We must have accurate information about Prophet Muhammad's life if we want to love as he did, to act in the way he did. To this end, the next section contains a summary of the Prophet's life.

PROPHET MUHAMMAD
A Short Biography

P rophet Muhammad was born on 20 April 571, on a Monday, in Makka. His father's name was Abd Allah, his mother's name was Amina, his paternal grandfather was Abd al-Muttalib, his maternal grandfather was called Wahb, his paternal grandmother was Fatima, and his maternal grandmother was Barra. The midwives who assisted at the birth were Shifa and Fatima. Umm Ayman assisted them. According to the midwives, at the time of Prophet Muhammad's birth, the house was filled with light.

The last Prophet was the fruit of Prophet Abraham's prayer, Jesus' glad tidings, and his mother Amina's dream. After building the Ka'ba, Prophet Abraham prayed to God "Our Lord! Raise up among that community a Messenger of their own, reciting to them Your Revelations, and instructing them in the Book (You will send to him) and the Wisdom, and purifying them (of false beliefs and doctrines, and sins, and all kinds of filth.) Surely, You are the All-Honored with irresistible might, the All-Wise."[3] Jesus told those around him of the Prophet who would follow him called "Ahmad." Prophet Muhammad's mother, Amina, had a dream in which she was told the following:

> "You are pregnant with the blessing of humanity and the leader of this community. Take shelter in God, the one and only, to protect him from jealousy and evil after he comes to this world, and later call him Ahmad or Muhammad."

The Prophet's birth was a sign of the acceptance of this prayer, the manifestation of these glad tidings, and the realization of this dream.

The Prophet's father, before the Prophet had even come into the world, had departed for another city for reasons of trade, became ill and died, and was buried in Madina. Thus, Prophet Muhammad never saw his father. From the time of his birth until he was four years old, he stayed with his wet-nurse, Halima. He then stayed for another two years with his mother Amina. When he was six, his mother took him to Madina to meet his relatives and to visit his father's grave. Because Salma, the mother of the Prophet's grandfather, Abd al-Muttalib, was from Madina, they had relatives in this city. The grave of Prophet Muhammad's father was in the garden of his uncles' house in Nabiga. Amina visited the grave of her husband, Abdullah, and the Prophet became acquainted with his relatives from the Najjar tribe. On the return journey, Amina became ill and died in a place called Abwa. She was buried there. Umm Ayman brought the Prophet to Makka and gave him into his grandfather's care. He stayed with his grandfather from the age of six until he was eight. When the Prophet's grandfather died, according to his will, Muhammad went to stay with his paternal uncle, Abu Talib. Abu Talib was a respected person in Makka, and he was known as the most esteemed of Abd al-Muttalib's sons.

Prophet Muhammad experienced all this loss when he was a child. Yet it did not destroy his fortitude. He herded his uncle's sheep to pasture in Makka. He carried every task at home with great joy and contributed to the family budget. His aunt, Fatima, treated him as her own and he never upset her. In those years, wherever the Prophet was living, even the house of his wet-nurse, found itself in plenty. As a matter of fact, although Abu Talib was not a wealthy person in those years, after the Prophet came to stay, it became apparent that he was a source of blessings for the household.

When he turned 13 he began to work, joining his uncles in trade. He was involved in trade for many years, and became known for his honesty and principles. When he was only 20, he joined an institution called *Hilf al-Fudl* (the alliance of the virtuous) set up by some Makkan people to combat thieves, robbers, brigands, oppression, and injustice; he was a very effective member. When he was 25, he married Khadija. Khadija was forty at that time and her decision to marry him was influenced primarily by his reputation as *"al-Amin"* (the trustworthy, the honest). When he was 35, he arbitrated in the reconstruction of the Ka'ba; there was a disagreement when it came time to place the Black Stone (*Hajar al-Aswad*) back in the Ka'ba, concerning which tribe should have the honor of performing this task. The Prophet put the stone on a ground cloth and had each tribe hold one corner, thus preventing certain conflict from arising among the tribes.

When the Prophet approached the age of forty, he experienced a desire to distance himself from people and to go out into the country to seek seclusion and to contemplate nature. He had lived an untainted childhood and youth. Now, looking back, he was deeply saddened by the corruption and amorality in the lives of the people around him. Because of this, he began to stay for certain periods in a cave called Hira on Mount Nur, near Makka. He would stay for a while and then return to the city. Once, on the return journey, he heard a voice call out "O, Muhammad!" from among the rocks and trees. It was subsequent to this that he started to have dreams that would be realized the next day.

When he was 40, in 610, during the month of Ramadan, the Archangel Gabriel came to him and the period of his revelations began. The first revelation was the verse that begins *Read, in the name of the Creator, God...* This is how Almighty God gave the duty of Prophethood to Muhammad.

The first people to accept the Prophet's invitation to Islam were Khadija, Ali, Zayd ibn Haritha and Abu Bakr. They were followed by Uthman, Abdurrahman ibn Awf, Sa'd ibn Abi Waqqas, Talha and Zubayr. Those first Muslims, in particular the Prophet, underwent great torment at the hands of the idol worshippers. In fact, many Muslims, like Yasir and his wife, Sumayya, were murdered after unbearable tortures. Bilal al-Habashi, Abu Fukayha, Habbab ibn Arat, and Umm Abis, Nahdiyya and Zinnira also underwent great torment. These were people who were held in low esteem by the idolaters; even the slaves and servants of these Muslims underwent many hardships.

The resistance of these first Muslims greatly affected the spread of Islam. As a matter of fact, during the first six years of the Prophethood, strong and brave men like Hamza and Umar embraced Islam and found their place among the Companions of the Prophet. As the number of those who believed in Islam increased, so did the number of obstacles placed by the idolaters to prevent the spread of this new faith. In the fifth and sixth year of the Prophethood, some Muslims were forced by the situation to attain permission from the Prophet to emigrate to Abyssinia. In the seventh year the unbelievers isolated the Muslims in one area and boycotted them. They were banned from trade, travel, and interrelations with other people. This situation lasted for three years. In the tenth year of the Prophethood, with the successive deaths of Khadija and Abu Talib, the torment and suffering caused by the enemies of Islam increased yet again. Khadija and Abu Talib were respected people in the community and this respect had, to some extent, provided a degree of protection for the Prophet. At this time, Prophet Muhammad went to Taif to try to gain some outside support. But the people of Taif not only did not accept Islam or give support to the Prophet, they stoned him, and he was only able to save himself by sheltering in an orchard outside Taif, covered in his own blood. In his supplication after having undergone this horrible treatment, the Prophet said that if he were truly fulfilling his mission then such torture meant nothing to him. It is without a doubt that he acted correctly and that he fulfilled his responsibilities.

At this time, those who ruled Makka reached a decision that he should not be allowed back into the city. For this reason, he turned to Mut'im ibn Adiyy to attain protection to enter Makka. It was a commonly observed tradition at those times among the prominent people of the Quraysh tribe that one could ensure security by attaining their protection.

While these successive torments were raining down on his head, Prophet Muhammad was taken by God on the heavenly journey, Mi'raj; this took him to the presence of Almighty God and he was blessed to receive divine commandments without a mediator. It was on this night that the Prophet brought down many of the rules that are found in sura Isra, the seventeenth chapter of the Qur'an; 12 of the commandments found between the 22 and 39 verses of sura Isra were revealed on this night. For a list of these commandments see section "The Three Months."

The bestowal of such a wonderful miracle through Prophet Muhammad was a sign that, sooner or later, Islam would flourish.

Despite all the difficulties, Prophet Muhammad's efforts to spread the message of Islam continued. He intensified most of his efforts on the crossroads where travelers from outside the city might pass. Finally, a group of six people who had come from Madina (then Yathrib) for pilgrimage testified the truth of the message he brought and promised to fulfill the conditions of Islam. The following year, five of this group came together with seven other people from Madina and gave their pledge to the Prophet at Aqaba. A second pledge took place with seventy-five people the next year, who promised to protect the Prophet as they protected their women and children. In the time that followed this, with the permission of Allah and that of the Prophet, the Muslims who were suffering in Makka emigrated to Madina. This is known as the *Hijra* in Islamic literature. The last to emigrate were the Prophet and Abu Bakr. This was a very difficult emigration, with the idolators of Makka chasing them from the Thawr caves to the south of Makka, and continuing pursuit until they had almost reached Madina. The Prophet and Abu Bakr traveled in great danger, but in the end, they managed to reach Madina. The Madinan people, in contrast to the Makkans, took the Prophet to their bosoms. They united around him. The people of Madina supported those who had abandoned their homes in Makka for the glory of God. It is for this reason that Almighty God calls the people of Madina the *Ansar* (the helpers) in the Qur'an. As a matter of fact, brother and sisterhood was established between the emigrants and the *Ansar* immediately after the emigration of the Prophet. In this way, the action of helping people gained a spiritual dimension. This support helped to waylay psychological problems. The emigrants found the opportunity to share their experience of Islam with the people of Medina. The emigrants established shops and markets, and they were able to support themselves in a very short time. In this way, the Muslims benefited the economic life of the city.

All of these events frightened the idolators in Makka. They wanted to destroy the Muslims before they became any stronger. The result was battles between the Muslims and the idolaters, like Badr, Uhud, the Battle of the Trench, and Muraysi. In the year 630, Makka was conquered. The Prophet returned in triumph to the city from which he had been driven. The purpose behind this return was to cleanse the Ka'ba from idols, and to revert the Ka'ba, built by Prophet Abraham, and the surrounding areas, to as it was intended to be. The Prophet did not act in revenge; he did not act with resentment. Rather, he issued a general pardon. He showed his greatness by forgiving when he was strong. He was planning unification, a celebration, and he had no time to waste on trivial matters. As a matter of fact, the muezzin of the Prophet, Bilal al-Habashi, by calling noon prayer from the roof of the Ka'ba, announced the superiority of unity and of one God to the skies of Makka.

The proud and haughty tribe of Hawazin, who could not stomach these new developments, laid plans to prevent the development of the Muslims; these plans were unsuccessful. They were defeated in their war against the Muslims. As a result, Islam resounded throughout the region, starting from the Hijaz region, and stretching throughout the Arabian Peninsula. Within one year after the Prophet had returned to Madina he hosted the representatives from hundreds of tribes.

In 632, during the time of the Hajj, the Prophet spoke before more than one hundred thousand Muslims. Known as the

Farewell Sermon, this speech was a summary of Islamic thought and presented the most perfect principles in human rights.

The beloved Prophet, who was able to communicate the message entrusted to him thanks to his patience, determination, and bravery, closed his eyes to this world on June 8, 632, a Monday.

The period in which the Prophet lived is known as the Age of Happiness, and the Blessed Era. During this Blessed Era, a generation known as the Companions came into being, made up, for the most part, of Emigrants (*muhajirun*) and the Helpers (*ansar*). This generation was made up of people who were firm in their faith, knowledgeable, well-mannered, masterful, hardworking, patient, and skilled, and they became role models to guide future generations.

FRIDAY, THE BLESSED DAY

Before examining the importance of the blessed day, Friday, for Muslims, we should look at the commandment given by Almighty God concerning Friday Prayer. In the Qur'an, God command Muslims in the following way:

> O, you who believe! When the call is made for Prayer on Friday, then hasten earnestly to the remembrance of God (by performing the Prayer and listening to the sermon), and leave off business (and every other thing). That is better for you, if you but know. And when the Prayer has been performed, then disperse abroad in the land and seek (your portion) of God's grace, but (without ever forgetting Him,) mention God much (whether during Prayer or not), so that you may prosper (in both worlds). (Juma 62:9-10)

This verse offers evidence from the Qur'an that Friday prayer is compulsory.

Friday is a very precious and holy day. On this matter, the Prophet gave the following orders:

> "We (Muslims) are the last (to come) but (will be) the foremost on the Day of Resurrection though the former nations were given the Holy Scriptures before us. And this was their day (Friday), the celebration of which was made compulsory for them but they differed about it. So God gave us the guidance for it (Friday), and all the other people are behind us in this respect: the Jews' (holy day is) tomorrow (i.e. Saturday), and the Christians' (is) the day after tomorrow (i.e. Sunday)."[4]

> "Adam was created on that day, he was sent down from Heaven on that day, his penitence was accepted on that day, he died on that day, and on that day will be the Day of Judgment. Every creature but humanity and the Jinn wait attentively—with the fear of the Hour—from dawn to sunrise. There is an

hour on that day when if a Muslim prays on a Friday, and hits upon the right hour, if they ask for a need to be fulfilled, God will certainly give it."[5]

"There is an hour on Friday that if a Muslim should pray at that hour, and hit the right hour, then if he desires a blessing from God, God will certainly grant it."[6]

Relying on the significance given to Fridays in such hadiths, it has been said, "Friday is the measure of the week, Ramadan the measure of the year, and the hajj the measure of one's lifetime." That is, if one prays Friday prayer in full consciousness of all that it means, then one is more likely to experience for a whole week the abundance and blessings that arise from it; if this is repeated every Friday, then one's life will become thus. Those Muslims who observe the month of Ramadan in the same fashion are then able to make all the months and days sources of abundance. Those Muslims who are able to make the pilgrimage, if they pray in sincerity, will be forgiven their sins; and if they make use of the spiritual light that shines during the pilgrimage, then they will have a life full of happiness.

It has been said that, "The hour on Friday when prayers and wishes are accepted is similar to the Night of Power during Ramadan."

It is considered a good action for a Muslim to take a full bath (*ghusl*) on Friday, to clean the parts of the body that need to be cleaned, to brush the teeth, to put on a light, pleasant scent, to wear clean clothes, and to smile and be pleasant. The Prophet said to those villagers who came from outside Madina "I wish that you keep yourself clean on this day of yours (i.e. take a bath)."[7] Muslims should cleanse themselves both spiritually and physically, becoming completely clean.

The Prophet told us that those Muslims who make *wudu* (ritual washing for prayers) carefully and go to the mosque to pray on Fridays, who listen carefully to the sermon, and pray on two successive Fridays, would be forgiven the sins they had committed in between.[8]

Of course, we must understand this in the correct way. From the very start, it must be stated that Muslims should be in the right spiritual state on this day, that they should pray and repent, that their prayers and penitence should be sincere, and that they should try to perform these at the correct hour. They should read the Qur'an and think about what is being said, and they should invoke God's blessings and peace upon the Prophet. Thus, any prayer, penitence, or repentance that one has tried to perform at the correct hour will be carried out in peace. Finally, Muslims who have sincerely prayed Friday prayer in accordance with this statement of the Prophet will leave the mosque with their soul purified of evil, with a clean heart and clean feelings, and return to their work or home.

At the morning prayer, on Friday the Prophet always read verses from sura Sajda and sura Insan from the Qur'an. The reason for this was that these verses include events that had happened or will happen on a Friday. These verses acted like a Friday breeze, bringing to people such events as the creation of Adam, a description of the Day of Judgment, and the resurrection of people in the other world, all working together to revitalize the faith of the listeners. In Sajda, for example, after telling people that God Almighty had sent the Qur'an as a reminder, the creation of the Heavens and the Earth is described:

> Apart from Him, you have no guardian to whom you can ultimately refer your affairs, and no intermediary agent that can cause anything of use to reach you without His leave. Will you not think and take heed? (Sajda 32:4)

The Qur'an also touches on the creation of human beings here and warns us:

> . . . and He endows you with the sense of hearing and eyes and innermost sense of perception. How scarcely you give thanks." (Sajda 32:9)

The chapter goes on to tell us how those who have perverted the way and who deny the Day of Judgment will be full of regrets in the other world after this day:

> If you could but see those criminals (who deny the Hereafter and are) lost in harvesting sin when they hang their heads before their Lord, pleading: "Our Lord! Now we see the truth and are able to hear, and are ready to obey. So please return us to the world: we will certainly do good, righteous deeds only. Now we are certain of the truth." (Sajda 32:12)

> Who is greater in doing wrong than he who has repeatedly been reminded of his Lord's Revelations and signs, yet turns away from them? (Sajda 32:22)

On the other hand, those who believe in God's verses humbly prostrate as they are counseled, give thanks to God, pleading with Him in fear and hope and spending of their own sustenance on the way to God. In return for this awaits happiness.

At the end of the chapter, God calls out to those who refuse to listen:

> Is it not enough as a means of guidance for them (the unbelievers) how many a generation We have destroyed before them, amidst whose dwelling places they travel? Surely in this are manifest signs. Will they still not lend an ear to their messages and the revealed warnings?
> Do they not consider that We drive the rain to the dry land, bare of herbage, and bring forth with it crops of which their cattle and they themselves eat? Will they still not see the truth?" (Sajda 32:26-27)

In the first verse of sura Insan, after stating that humans are created from sperm, God states that he gave them sight and hearing and that the true path has been shown to them. According to the rest of the chapter, human beings have been put on this Earth as a test; some are grateful while others are ungrateful. God Almighty describes the eternal reward that awaits those who do good on the Day of Judgment.

Whereas, the truly pious and godly will drink from a cup filled to the brim with heavenly wine flavored with heavenly additives. A spring of which God's servants will drink to the full satiation, causing it to gush forth abundantly and to whatever direction they want. (God's truly pious and godly servants are they who) fulfill all the responsibilities they undertake, and fear a Day whose woes are bound to spread far and wide and encompass (whomever it will encompass). They give food, however great be their need for it, with pleasure to one who is destitute or an orphan or a captive, "We feed you only for God's sake and to obtain His good pleasure; we desire from you neither a reward nor thanks. Actually, We fear on account of our Lord a Day that is extremely frowned (on) and harsh (toward criminals)." So, certainly God will preserve them from the woes of that Day and will make them welcomed with their faces bright with happiness and themselves joyful. He will reward them for all that they have endured with a Garden (of Paradise) and garments of silk, reclining therein on raised, adorned couches. They will find therein neither burning sun nor severe cold. And its shadows will come down low over them, and its clusters of fruit will hang down low within their reach. And they will be served from vessels of silver and goblets that seem to be crystal, crystal-clear, made of silver—they themselves determine the kind and amount of the drink, as they wish. And there they will be given to drink of a cup flavored with the ginger (of Paradise), (filled from) a spring therein which is called Salsabil (as it flows smoothly and continuously as they wish)." (Insan 76:5-18)

After completing the description of the reward that awaits them in Heaven, the remainder of the verse goes on to state how all this beauty will be given in return for the efforts of human beings.

So wait patiently for your Lord's judgment, and be not mindful of the (caprices and offers of) any who are sinful and insistent on unbelief among them. And mention the Name of your Lord, (worship Him) in the early morning and in the afternoon. And in a part of night prostrate for Him, and glorify Him for a long part of the night. (Insan 76:24-26)

After reminding us of these, the Qur'an goes on to underline an important reality:

> Truly, those (sinful unbelievers) love and prefer that which is in
> advance (the present life of the world), and completely neglect
> a grievous Day before them. (Insan 76:27)

Friday and Friday prayer are two great signs and symbols of
Islam. On the day before the Eid of Sacrifice all the believers gather on Arafat as a part of the pilgrimage rituals; as a requirement
of Islam, one day a year, a huge crowd gathers there. Other than
this one day, Muslims come together to pray either the Eids or
Fridays. Friday has a particular importance, as Muslims come together on that day every week, allowing them to experience the joy
of an Eid each week.

Friday is an important day to have one's heart enlightened. It
is on this day that one is expected to attain a higher level of understanding of what Islam is about.

Muslims usually pray for peace and blessings upon the Prophet
on Friday more than on any other day of the week. This is how
they show their gratitude to the one to whom they are indebt-
ed for the security their belief offers and the happiness of Islam.
Gifts and favors from God will be given on Friday, and the final
reckoning will take place on that day. The *Mazid Day*, when the
believers enter Heaven and are showered with God's blessing
will also be a Friday.

Moreover, in this world, Friday is a festival for Muslims and
those who sincerely stretch out their hands to God will not be
turned away; the hour of the *ijaba* (the hour when prayers and
wishes are accepted) is on that day.

It has been reported in a hadith that the Prophet himself
recommended Muslims to ask blessings for him on Friday, as he
was to be presented with greetings on that day.

Those who read the sura Kahf on Fridays have been given the
glad tidings of heavenly rewards. It is stated that Friday prayer
is atonement for any sins committed since the previous Friday.

Any charity given to the needy on a Friday will bring great rewards. Friday is a day of preaching and advice. The sermons after Friday prayers shine a light on important matters for Muslims, providing everyone with a spiritual light by which they are able to correct their errors and to make up for any deficiencies.

If one analyses the worship on Friday and the psychology of this day from a scientific view, a very important conclusion can be arrived at. The penitence, remembrance, prayers, and greetings of the night before Friday continue during the day in preparation for the noon-prayer, for the sermon and advice after the prayer, and in the search for the *ijaba* hour; all these bring the servant of God into an extremely sensitive state. If this condition is repeated every week, then that person's positive emotions are developed, while their negative emotions are lessened. In this way, Friday prayer, with all that comes before and after it, is a means of spiritual education.

It would be appropriate to look at one last point concerning Friday. It can now be understood, thanks to the matters explained above and the evidence given, that the day and night of Friday need to be spent in a more aware state of mind. But it would not be right to perform supererogatory prayers on Friday alone, and neglect the other days of the week, or to not carry out a supererogatory fast, fasting only on Friday. But there is no objection to performing a supererogatory prayer on Friday if the same has been done on other days of the week, nor to perform a supererogatory fast if this has been done on the other days of the week.[9]

This warning tells us that Muslims should not only act in awareness on certain days and nights of the week, but they should act this way every day and every night.

FASTING ON CERTAIN DAYS

According to Aisha, the Prophet would perform supererogatory fasts on days that did not fall in Ramadan. But these supererogatory fasts were not all performed in one month. He would fast on some days of the month, while he would not on others. More light can be shed on the matter if one examines the hadiths concerning this matter as reported by the Companions. Aisha, the Mother of Believers, who was the best observer of the Prophet on this matter, said:

> The Prophet would sometimes fast until we commented on the fact that he hadn't had an iftar (fast-breaking meal) that month. Sometimes he wouldn't fast until we commented that he had not as yet fasted that month. I have never seen the Prophet fast as much as he did in Ramadan in any other month. Shaban was the month that he fasted in most (after Ramadan).[10]

Again according to Aisha, the Prophet ordered his Companions to:

> Take on as much worship as you have strength to do. Even if you get tired of your worship, God Almighty never tires of giving blessings . . . according to God, the best effort is that which is continuous, even if it is little.[11]

I think this matter will become clearer if we look at a hadith concerning the supererogatory prayers and how to carry them out. This hadith was reported by Abd Allah, the son of Amr ibn al-As; he is the person involved in the situation that led to this hadith. He was known among the Companions for his piety. When the Prophet was told that he had sworn: "As long as I live I will spend my nights in prayer and my days fasting," he asked him if he had really said this. When he learned that this was the case, he said:

You will not be able to carry out such a strenuous form of worship, you won't be strong enough. (If you ask me), you should sometimes fast, sometimes eat. (Some nights) sleep, some nights pray. Fast three days of every month. God rewards every good and beneficial act or form of worship ten times as much as it is worth. (God) said, *Whoever comes into (God's) presence with goodness will get ten times more...*(Anam 6:160). Thus, if you fast three days every month it is as if you have fasted the whole year. (That is a person who fasts three days every month receives blessings as if they had fasted all year).

When Abd Allah said that he could handle more, the Prophet told him "Fast one day, and eat for two." But Abd Allah insisted that he could do even more, so the Prophet recommended that he follow the example of David, who would fast one day and eat the next. When Abd Allah still insisted that he could do more than this, the Prophet said "There is no greater fast than this."[12]

When Abd Allah ibn Amr had become old and found this method of fasting more and more difficult to adhere to he said, "I must admit that it would have been better for me to do as the Prophet said and to fast 3 days a month."[13]

What we can understand from the Prophet's advice is that a Muslim must act in full awareness in all religious matters. However, supererogatory forms of worship should not weaken the body, thus preventing one from carrying out physical, familial, or social responsibilities. It is more suitable to carry out smaller forms of worship, but to do these continuously. We are able to reach this conclusion by examining the Prophet's statement that there are benefits of fasting on some days. The following hadith underlines this fact. The Prophet said:

Fasting on three days every month and the whole month of Ramadan is the same as fasting for the whole year. As far as fasting on the eve of Eid, I hope that God will cover your sins of the previous and following years. If you fast on Ashura day I hope that this will atone for the sins of the year before.[14]

There are also similar sayings cited to the Prophet that fasting on Mondays and Thursdays was praiseworthy. In fact, according to Aisha, "Our Prophet tried to fast on Mondays and Thursdays."[15]

Similarly, it has been reported that the Prophet said the following concerning this matter:

> Mondays and Thursdays are the days of petition for actions (worship, behavior, and service). I am pleased to have my actions presented while fasting.[16]

A hadith narrated by Abu Hurayra tells us of the virtues of fasting in the month of Muharram:

> After Ramadan, of all the months the most virtuous month to fast is Muharram. After the obligatory (fard) prayers, the most virtuous prayers are those performed at night.[17]

There are reports that the Prophet recommended to some of the Companions that they fast for three days in each of the months of Rajab, Dhu al-Qada, Dhu al-Hijja, and Muharram.[18]

What all of these show us is that the Prophet did not put any burdensome supererogatory forms of worship on the believers, but rather introduced forms that would help to revitalize their belief. Again, we can understand that the amount of supererogatory worship suggested by the Prophet was not so great as to create stress or weariness, but rather that it was within the bounds of physical, familial, and social responsibilities, and that it consisted of forms of worship that could be continuously carried out.

THE THREE MONTHS

In the calendar that dates from the emigration of the Prophet (*hijra*) the months of Rajab, Shaban, and Ramadan are popularly known as the holy and blessed months. The expression "The Three Months" can be said to express the virtues inherent in these months.

According to theological literature and to oral tradition, the main reason for the three months being a time of virtue is that the times of the blessed nights of Raghaib and Mi'raj fall in Rajab, the Bara'a in Shaban, and the Night of Power in Ramadan.

In this chapter we will give information about these nights that give honor to the three months as we discuss the topic of the Three Months.

THE MONTHS OF RAJAB AND SHABAN

It must be said first that our example for finding the spiritual value of the three months has been taken, as with every matter, from Prophet Muhammad.

The Companions report that the months during which the Prophet fasted the most—other than Ramadan—were the months of Rajab, Shaban, Muharram, and Shawwal.

The Prophet prayed in the following manner at the beginning of the month of Rajab:

> "Oh God! Make Rajab and Shaban holy for us and bring us to Ramadan!"

The month of Shaban follows the month of Rajab. Aisha said "I did not see the Prophet fast as much in any other month as he did in the month of Shaban."[19]

In a conversation the Prophet had with one of the Companions, the importance of fasting during Shaban is reflected. This conversation is recorded as follows in the hadith:

> The Prophet addressed someone "Did you fast in the middle of this month (Shaban)?" When that individual answered, "No, I did not," the Prophet ordered him, "Then, after the last Ramadan fast (i.e. after the Eid) fast for two more days."[20]

THE SPECIAL CONDUCT OF THE PROPHET AND THE COMPANIONS IN THREE MONTHS

It can be understood from the hadith that the Prophet fasted more during the months of Rajab and Shaban and that he performed supererogatory prayers in addition to the compulsory ones, that his remembrance and glorification of God, prayers of thanks and gratitude would increase, and that he would give more in charity to the poor.

The Companions would strive with all their might to attain the blessings of these months. They would increase their supererogatory prayers, they would repent more and offer more penitence, they would give more to charity; they strove to make orphans, the lonely, the destitute, and the needy happy and comfortable. In particular, they would perform whatever deeds of charity they could to make this month, which preceded Ramadan, as happy and comfortable as possible for those who were in need.

Intense worship during the three months makes people more sensitive, helping to prevent negative behavior, increasing the feeling of charity in people, and increasing the awareness of the need to take care of and support those who are in need of help in society. In these months, people feel the need to be more aware of their servanthood, that they should try to perform more positive actions, and that they should perform more charitable deeds, giving greater importance to such matters. This is beneficial not only to individuals, but to the whole of society.

A psychological analysis of the effect that the three months have on the benefits to the moral education of the individual and society could produce some startling results.

RAGHAIB

The night preceding the first Friday of the month of Rajab is known as "Laylat al-Raghaib." This is one of the holy nights for Muslims.

The word Raghaib is the plural form of *ragiba*, which has meanings like "beautiful, valuable, a gift." Thus the phrase Laylat al-Raghaib means "A night full of grace and gifts, of great value, that should be observed in the proper way." It was on this night that the Prophet had attained many of God Almighty's graces and gifts, and therefore prayed in thanks, gratitude and penance.

There is an incorrect belief among people that this night was the night that the Prophet's mother, Amina, conceived him. His date of birth does not give any basis for such a belief. It is possible that this was the night that she realized that she was pregnant with the Prophet. It would be more appropriate to interpret this common belief in this way.

Even the very name of this night implies its spirituality and therefore makes clear that it is a night on which Muslims should behave in a becoming way. One of the blessings of this night must be that it acts as a herald for the holy month of Ramadan. The fact that the months of Rajab, Shaban, and Ramadan follow one another causes Muslims to act in a more controlled manner on the days of these months. Raghaib acts as a reminder that the month of Ramadan, that "prince of months" when one purifies oneself of the errors of one's heart, soul, and mind, is on its way. This is very important psychologically because those who immerse themselves in this state of mind are able to prepare their souls for the start; they scrutinize their daily worship, their charitable acts, their individual and familial responsibilities, and their services to society. In short, they put themselves through a spiritual audit that is very beneficial. This awakens the resolution and desire toward what is good and to purify the soul of what is bad.

MI'RAJ

Almighty God puts those of His servants who are to be rewarded with great things through a variety of tests. All the prophets have been through such tests. Prophet Muhammad went through trials, and despite all the great difficulties that he underwent he carried on the struggle to glorify God's name with resolution and effort. He never lost his conviction that, one day, Islam would be accepted by a great number of people. This is the reason why he prayed for the reform of the people of Makka and Taif, despite all the hardship they put him through.

The miracle of the Mi'raj (literally "ascension") occurred as he reached the pinnacle of his struggle, in an atmosphere of violent oppression from his enemies.

It is commonly accepted that the Mi'raj occurred one and a half years before the emigration to Madina (621), on the 26 or 27 of the month of Rajab. The Mi'raj is a miracle granted to the Prophet, where he was brought (or ascended) into the presence of God in a special form and nature and where he became a direct addressee of the revelation.

It is reported that first the Prophet rode on a mount called Buraq from the Masjid al-Haram (the Ka'ba in Makka) to the Masjid al-Aqsa in Jerusalem, and from there went with the Archangel Gabriel in a spiritual ascent to the Heavens, to the Sidrat al-Muntaha, the Lote Tree of the Furthest Limit. Gabriel left him there, and from there on the Prophet was accompanied by a servant called Rafraf, who took him on a journey unbounded by time, space, or direction into the presence of God.[21] The blessed phrases of the *tashahhud* or *tahiyyat* (the prayers recited while sitting in the daily prayers) were uttered by Almighty God and His Messenger in their sacred conversation.[22] The Prophet was commanded to relay the five daily prayers to the people; on his return he was shown the qualities of Heaven and Hell.

This trip in actuality lasted only a few seconds; the polytheists in Makka refused to believe the Prophet when he spoke about it, yet the Prophet was able to answer any questions put to him about Jerusalem correctly. He was even describing where a caravan that was returning from there could be found, yet they still refused to believe. Abu Bakr, on the other hand, upheld the Prophet's statements without hesitation and said, "If he says so, then it is true." He was given the title "Siddiq," by the Prophet, meaning "He who confirmed the truth without hesitation."

Sura Isra of the Qur'an indicates this event.xxiii. This chapter is a source of reference for the Mi'raj as it refers to the Prophet's journey from the Masjid al-Haram to the Masjid al-Aqsa. There is some dispute whether the Prophet prayed with all the prophets at the Temple in Jerusalem before the Mi'raj or after it.

All the prophets were blessed with a kind of "ascension," each at a different level, however the Mi'raj of Prophet Muhammad was the most exalted.

It is necessary to state here that the commandments given to humanity by God that were entrusted to the Prophet on that night are just as important as the way in which the Mi'raj happened. It would be appropriate to list the twelve orders handed down to us from God through the Prophet in order of importance:

1. To be a servant to no one but God
2. To treat one's parents well
3. To give rights to relatives, the poor, and travelers on the road
4. To avoid meanness and waste
5. Not to kill one's offspring in fear of poverty
6. To avoid adultery and fornication
7. Not to kill others
8. To approach the goods of orphans in an appropriate manner
9. To keep one's word
10. To be accurate with measures and weights
11. Not to pursue that of which you have no knowledge
12. Not to walk haughtily on the Earth. To avoid conceit[24]

These commandments were given at the time of the Mi'raj, at a rather early date of Islam (toward the end of the Makkan period). It is manifest through these commandments that Islam addresses all of life along with all its principles.

The command to worship none other than God emphasizes the oneness of God; the command to treat our parents, relatives, the poor, and travelers well shows us the necessity for social solidarity and cooperation; being warned off meanness and extravagance aims to point us toward the middle way, the economic way for which we should strive. The commandment forbidding us from killing our offspring in fear of poverty is based on the fact that God will give everyone what they need to stay alive; fornication and adultery are forbidden because these are things that tear at the fabric of society; taking the lives of others is forbidden because murder is one of the worst acts possible; abusing the property of an orphan or confiscating their property in an unjust manner is clearly forbidden; the keeping of one's word is given importance, because this is the only way people in a society can feel secure. The correct use of weights and measurements are emphasized to avoid suspicion or dishonest behavior, while to ensure that people understand the importance of having a sense of direction in life, we are forbidden from pursuing that of which we have no knowledge as well as being reminded to avoid conceit.

There were three gifts granted to the Muslim community on the night of Mi'raj:

1. The community of Muhammad was promised that those who did not associate partners with God, after paying for their sins, would be taken into Heaven.
2. The daily prayers were set at 5. The Prophet stated that daily prayers are the Mi'raj of every believer.
3. According to sources, the final two verses of sura al-Baqara were revealed that night with a multitude of glad tidings. In the first verse of this revelation, all the principles of belief are listed. This verse orders Muslims to believe in all the

previous prophets and their books, which is in fact a call for peace, understanding, and respect. It is because of the many verses like this in the Qur'an that Muslims believe that human beings have the potential, despite all the differences of religion and race, to establish peace on this Earth. Throughout history, Islamic states have based their policies on this verse, showing tolerance to non-Muslims, letting them live in peace. What this verse shows us is that everyone lives Islam according to their strength and ability. Those who are not strong enough will not be imposed upon. Thus, it is possible for Muslims of all decrees of intelligence and ability to live Islam.

The Mi'raj also was a herald of the Emigration of the Prophet. Thus the Mi'raj is a symbol of the rise of Islam, of its ability to overcome all obstacles, its dynamism to spread, the constant hope of its success, and the fact that it would eventually overcome all obstacles, with the help of God.

The Mi'raj was a reward for the Prophet, a reward for never refusing the test he was undergoing, despite all the problems; even though his life was threatened, he never gave up his belief that Islam would be accepted by a great number of people. It was for such devout belief and endurance that he was rewarded. The Prophet completely understood the message of the Mi'raj; his hope for the future of Islam, that great numbers of people would be Muslims, increased, and his efforts to this end redoubled with joy.

BARA'A

Bara'a occurs on the fifteenth night of Shaban and is celebrated with spiritual joy by Muslims.

This night has been given various titles, such as the *"The Blessed, Warrant,"* or *"The Edict."* It is called *Blessed* because it is a night of abundance, spiritual productivity, prosperity and holiness; it is known as *Bara'a* (acquittal or salvation) because it has been granted to Muslims by Almighty God as an opportunity to be puri-fied of sins and to free themselves from their wrongs, it is known as *Rank*—or *Record*—because those who have performed deeds that are deemed worthy (who have spent this night in an appro-priately aware manner) are chosen to be approved of by God Almighty, and *Mercy* because the Mercy of God is attained on this night.

The Meaning and Importance of Bara'a

The Qur'an states the following:

> By the Book that makes things clear; We sent down a blessed night; For We (ever) wish to warn (against Evil.) In that (night) is made distinct every affair of wisdom. (Duhan 44:1-4)

Some scholars have determined that the night discussed in this verse is that of the Night of Power, while others have seen it to be the Night of Bara'a. Other scholars have combined the two, coming up with the following interpretation:

> "The holiness of Bara'a is related to the revelation of the Qur'an on that night. On the fifteenth night of Shaban (i.e. the Night of Bara'a) was when the Qur'an was sent down to the skies of the world in a complete form; the Night of Power is when the Qur'an began to be written by the scribes in charge and revealed section by section to the Prophet through the mediation of Archangel Gabriel. For this reason, it is not a con-tradiction to interpret this verse (Duhan 44:1-4) as indicating the Night of Bara'a while the Night of Power marks the first night of revelation . . ."[25]

The Five Characteristics of This Night and the Matter of Intercession

In Islamic sources, as well as in popular culture, it is stated that there are five characteristics belonging to this night:

1. Though not found in the best authenticated sources, it is reported in a hadith narrated by Aisha that heavenly

decisions regarding those who will be born, those who will die, and the actions of people are placed in front of God, while their sustenance is revealed. However, this hadith is not considered reliable.

2. The forms of worship performed on that night (prayers, reading of the Qur'an, reciting of prayers, remembrance, and repentance) are greatly supported by the fasting and worshipping carried out on the previous day.

3. It is a night of abundance and blessings.

4. It is a night of forgiveness.

5. This was the night when our Prophet was granted intercession. On the thirteenth of Shaban Prophet Muhammad requested from Almighty God the right to intercede for his nation. On that night, he was granted the ability to intercede for 1/3 of Muslims; on the fourteenth he was granted another 1/3; while on the fifteenth, he once again made the same request and was granted intercession for all Muslims.

The following hadith concerning the fifteenth night of Shaban is of significance here:

> "When it is the middle of the month of Shaban, enliven the night with your prayers (spend that night in a way that is suitable to the spiritual meaning). Fast during the day, because God Almighty will descend to the Heavens of the earth at the time of sunset and say "Is there no one who is repentant? I will forgive them. Is there no one who wants a blessing? I will bless them. Is there no one who is ill? I will give them health. He will continue to ask "Is there no one. . .?" until morning."[26]

The Prophet recommended to some believers whom he knew had not fasted in the middle of Shaban (the night of Bara'a), to fast one or two days after Ramadan instead.[27]

An Important Opportunity for Muslims

God forgives every servant who turns to Him, who bows his or her head in repentance, or who weeps over mistakes; this is what the Night of Bara'a clearly announces with blessings, abundance, and gifts. It calls on Muslims to take stock of and consider their actions. On the other hand, it would be highly inappropriate to remain impervious to the call of the Prophet who prayed to God to accept his intercession on the behalf of all believers.

According to Islamic sources, those who are "practicing witch-craft, seeking revenge, abusing alcohol and drugs to become intoxicated and not trying to free themselves from these, those who do not treat their parents appropriately, and those who adhere to adultery, will not be able to avail themselves of the forgiveness, blessings, and intercession of this night. While it is possible for every-one to avail themselves of these blessings, there will be some who remain outside this mercy. Those who try to eliminate the bad characteristics inherent in themselves, who examine their actions, who take this opportunity with their heart and mind fully aware, and who try to eliminate all evil in themselves are those who can benefit. It is an opportunity as well for those who say "I am immersed in sin; there is no hope for my salvation." These people will turn to God, run to the mosque, mingle with the congrega-tion, worship, listen to the Qur'an, pray, and plead for divine for-giveness. Those who act in such a way on this night will have tast-ed this spiritual atmosphere, they will have purged the evil, dis-tanced themselves from sin, adopted feelings of goodness, and turned toward good behavior; thus they will be able to reach the Infinite Mercy.

What To Do on the Blessed Days and Nights

1. If conditions and health permit, Muslims should go to the mosque on blessed days and nights and pray with the congregation. Thus, not only will they be able to earn more blessings, but they will also have the chance to come together with their workmates and neighbors to share in this prosperous atmosphere.

2. On these days and nights, great spiritual meaning can be achieved by young people if they go to the mosque along

with their elders. They can better understand the importance of being part of a congregation, of solidarity, of cooperation, and togetherness in such a joyful environment.

3. The effort to meet with neighbors and friends on the blessed days and nights provides an opportunity to make a positive contribution in sharing the joy and sadness, the success and problems of loved ones, as Muslims go out of their way to ask people how they are at these times.

4. A Muslim should strive to read the Qur'an, listen to it, join in talks concerning the Qur'an and hadiths, listen to sermons, and pay attention to religious advice; these all lead to a spiritual atmosphere that helps to create a sense of peace in people. Muslims should spend time thinking about what is said in the Qur'an and the hadiths, they should strive to make up for any gaps in their religious knowledge, and to deepen that which they already have.

5. Remembrance, repentance, and penitence to God on such days and nights deepen a Muslim's awareness of his or her servanthood.

6. It is easier to approach Almighty God during prayer on the holy days and nights; people are closest to God when they are praying, which is the greatest form of remembrance. It is beneficial to pay particular attention to one's worship on these days and nights.

7. It is necessary to pray sincerely to God on such days to protect all of humanity and to strengthen the bonds within the community, to ensure security and peace, to protect all people from disasters. Thus, a person is able to become aware of themselves as a beneficial member of the human race.

8. Muslims should take stock of his servanthood on such days. How are they fulfilling their duties as parents, sons or daughters, businesspeople, teachers, students, directors, or citizens? They should identify their mistakes and faults in a form of auto-criticism, and then be determined and hopeful that he will be more useful and more successful.

RAMADAN

The ninth month of the Islamic year, Ramadan, is the obligatory month of fasting, and every Muslim who has the duty of fasting (some are relieved of this obligation due to illness or for other reasons) should abstain from food, drink, and sexual pleasure during the hours of daylight. The first day of the tenth month, Shawwal, marks the end of the fast and is a day of great rejoicing. Concerning the order to fast, the Qur'an declares:

> The month of Ramadan, in which the Qur'an (began to be) sent down as a pure source of guidance for people, and, (when practiced,) as clear signs of guidance and the Criterion (between truth and falsehood). Therefore, whoever of you is present at this month must fast it, and he who is so ill that he cannot fast or is on a journey must fast the same number of other days. God desires ease for you, and desires not hardship for you, so that you can complete the number of the days required, exalt God for that He has guided you, and it is hoped that you may give thanks (due to Him). (Baqara 2:185)

According to the Qur'an, the fasting hours are as follows:

> Eat and drink until you can discern the white streak (of dawn) against the black streak (of night); then complete the fast until night sets in. (Baqara 2:187)

Thus, the fast should start when the first thread of light is visible at dawn (between one and a half, or two hours before sunrise, depending on the time of year), and be maintained until sunset (the beginning of the night).

Ramadan is a month of blessings, and its most distinctive rituals are the predawn meal (*sahur*), the fast-breaking meal (*iftar*), and the special congregational prayers held after the *iftar* (*tarawih*).

There are several sayings of Prophet Muhammad concerning this month:

"During Ramadan the doors to mercy are opened, the doors to Hell are fastened, and the devils are struck with chains."[28]

"During Ramadan the doors of mercy are opened, the doors to Hell are fastened and the devils are beaten with chains."[29]

Prophet Muhammad recommended that Muslims partake of the predawn meal:

"Eat *sahur*. There is blessing in this."[30]

It is advised that the fast-breaking meal be eaten quickly.

"People who break fast quickly (observing the Prophet's tradition) always live an auspicious life."[31]

As reported by the Companions, "The Prophet would break his fast quickly and pray the evening prayer quickly; he never delayed these."[32]

In some Muslim societies, people who go to the mosques for evening prayer take a light meal along with them, like cheese, olives, etc. When the call for evening prayer is heard, they share this food with the other people in the mosque, and then pray together.

The practice of breaking fast quickly can be observed in those who go on the minor pilgrimage (*umra*) during Ramadan in Makka and Madina. Millions of Muslims prepare a practical meal, and sit in the environments of the Grand Mosque, the Ka'ba, and the Masjid al-Nabi, eating dates, and drinking Zamzam water (water from the blessed well near Ka'ba), and then proceed to pray as a congregation.

Let us look at the month of Ramadan and its spiritual characteristics more closely.

One day, when Prophet Muhammad went up to Sa'd ibn Ubada, the latter took out a piece of bread and some olives. The Prophet ate these. Later he said, "May those who are fasting have *iftar* at your tables, may good people partake, and may the angels pray for you."[33]

Prophet Muhammad told us:

> "If a person invites a fasting person to iftar, they will earn blessings as if they have fasted without any decrease on the blessings of the one who fasted."[34]

It is reported that *tarawih* prayer during Ramadan, a prayer that comes between night (*isha*) prayer and the *witr* prayer, is a means for people to be forgiven their sins. Prophet Muhammad said the following on this matter:

> "If a person prays on the holy nights of Ramadan, believing in its blessings and hoping for reward only from God, praying tarawih prayer for His pleasure, they will be forgiven their past sins."[35]

> "The person who, believing in the virtue and reward of the action, prays to God on the nights of Ramadan will be forgiven past minor sins."[36]

The following hadith describes how blessed fasting in Ramadan is and how fasting is much more than limiting what one eats and drinks, but is also the control of one's hands, tongue and eyes; during Ramadan, Muslims should not criticize or gossip about others.

> "Almighty God said: 'Any good deeds or form of worship performed by a human being (has an idea) of self-benefit. But fasting is not like this. Fasting is done purely for Me. Only I give the reward.' Fasting is like a shield. When one is fasting one should not use bad words, or scream and shout. If another person swears or tries to fight with you, just say 'I'm fasting!' 'I swear by God, with whom the soul of Muhammad resides, that the breath of one who is fasting will smell the sweetest of all on the Day of Judgment.' There are two important joys that grant relief for the person who fasts; the relief of iftar at dusk and the relief and joy of the reward given by God for fasting on one's return to Him."[37]

Prophet Muhammad told believers that a special door will be opened for those who fast sincerely during the month of Ramadan:

> "There is a door to Heaven known as Rayyan. Only those who have fasted can go through that door on the Day of Judgment. No one but they may enter. On the Day of Judgment, when it is announced, "Where are those who fasted?" those who fasted will stand up and go in. After the last of those who has fasted has entered, the door will close, and no one (except those who fasted) will have been able to enter."[38]

GENEROSITY AND READING THE QUR'AN

According to a report from the Companions: "The Prophet was the most generous of men. In particular, during Ramadan, when he met with Angel Gabriel, he was extremely generous. Gabriel would meet up with the Prophet every night of Ramadan and they would take turns to read the Qur'an. Thus, through these meetings of Gabriel and the Prophet, the breeze of mercy was more generous, more beneficial."[39]

The two things mentioned above are generosity and the reading of the Qur'an. These two aspects found in the hadith are widespread traditions of Ramadan, found throughout the Islamic world and throughout our country. Throughout the world, sincere Muslims are more generous, kind, and more receptive in their hearts during Ramadan. Those who are in a financially sound position go out of their way to help those who are not. Ramadan is the month of the Qur'an. The reading of the entire Qur'an during the month of Ramadan is prevalent in both mosques and private homes. The *hafiz*s (those who have memorized the Qur'an) read the Qur'an in gentle tones, and those who are listening carefully follow along. The 30 *juz*s (one part of the Qur'an) are read, this is called a *khatm*, and then there is a group prayer. In this way, people have the opportunity to bask their souls, frayed with stress and worry, in the light of the Qur'an and to luxuriate in its peaceful climate.

ITIKAF—DEVOTION TO PRAYER

Again, as reported by the Companions, the Prophet tells us about the custom of *itikaf* (shutting oneself away) during the last ten days of Ramadan. The Night of Power, a night more blessed than a thousand months, falls in the last ten days of Ramadan, which is actually the main reason for many Muslims to retreat for *itikaf*.

Itikaf means to stay in the mosque, or some area connected to the mosque, for the purpose of prayer. In this way, people can distance themselves from worldly life and approach closer to God; they are able to make an effort to deepen their religious feelings, to take stock of their human failings (examining their *nafs*), and they can try to attain divine pleasure and abundance.

Aisha informed us of how the Prophet would pass the last ten days of Ramadan in the following way:

> "When we were in the last ten days of Ramadan, the Prophet would enliven the nights with his prayer more than at other times; he would wake up family members to prayer, he would give more attention to worship, and he would put more effort into his prayers and worship than at other times."[40]

RAMADAN—A THOUGHT-PROVOKING MONTH

The Ramadan fast for those who believe in its blessings and who hope for its rewards acts as a complete guide and educator. Ramadan is a month of forgiveness, divine favors, and grace. In connection with these, those believers who open their hands in sincerity before the throne of All-Merciful God, those who repent their sins, will be forgiven; their hearts will be filled with happiness, their faces will be blessed with a smile, and waves of generosity will ceaselessly flow into their hands.

Hearts are revived in Ramadan, the soul is awakened, the brain clarified, the spirit purified, perception cleansed, and the will sharpened. The Muslim is armored against all wickedness, sins, forbidden things and those material things that pose a threat to the spirit.

In this month, the intellect has been enlightened by the never-ending light of the revelation, by the glory of the Qur'an, and by the tenderness of the Sunna.

It is not only stomachs that remain hungry in Ramadan. Those who stay hungry, but whose tongues spin lies, swear and slander, who gossip and who by so doing stab this or that person in the back, those who spread their poison—these people, while their stomachs remain hungry, their heart, the seat of belief, becomes a forge of mischief and treachery. These people have left nothing but tiredness and pain. But fasting should not be like this; the fasting tongue should say something good or say nothing at all. The fasting tongue should utter God's name and pray; it should utter words that are good and helpful. Groundless fears, misgivings, doubts, mischief, and treachery should leap from the heart, the seat of belief. In their place should come conscious belief and mature morality. Tricks springing from avarice and defeatist thoughts will flee from the mind.

The Muslim who performs the fast so that it is accepted as a form of worship fasts not only with their stomach; their hands, tongue, and heart also fast . . . all the organs of the body share the blessings of the fast, adopting the same goal.

Fasting is the source of our self-examination; it creates an atmosphere of deep thought. The Ramadan sky is always full of clouds that are ready to send down a rain of mercy. The hearts that have become barren through neglect turn verdant in this rain; the hand, the tongue, and the heart work together under the merciful clouds, finding one another, taking joy in each other's company.

Fasting is a chance provided for us to eliminate the disorder and defects found within us. This is a month of refreshment for our tired physical organs. Breezes of generosity waft through our hands, orphans smile, the poor are made happy, and the elderly are given hope and happiness in this month.

The believers, whose internal worlds are at peace and ordered, stretch out their hands to the stranger, to the needy, to the desperate. Some give money, some give tenderness, some give sympathy, some give love to these needy people; the smile on a face that has forgotten how to smile lights up the world.

This month has the spiritual potential to meet all that is expected of it—this month is the cure for all troubles.

Ramadan is a physician who possesses the cure for those who sincerely worship God, for those who worship God without hypocrisy—for the servant who sincerely presents his or her servanthood to God.

RAMADAN AND A CHANGING SOCIETY

Ramadan has a great influence on many social aspects in a Muslim society. Along with personal spiritual training, it has many communal dimensions. Muslims usually prefer to pay their annual obligatory charity or alms (*zakat*) during this month since it is more rewarding than if given at other times of the year. Therefore, this month takes on yet another dimension for the poor. This is a time of rejoicing for them; Muslims are told, *"He who sleeps well while his neighbor is hungry is not a true believer."*

In particular, there is the *Sadaqa al-Fitr* (the charity of fast-breaking) that is given during Ramadan; this is a tax that compels those who are considered to be well off according to the religious rules to give to the poor. In this way, caring about the poor ceases to be a matter of charity or pity, but rather becomes a social duty and responsibility.

Moreover, when one looks at the matter from the point of education, Ramadan is an important opportunity to help those who have fallen victim to the vices of drinking, smoking, and gambling; it also helps draw children away from these and teaches them good habits. It is amazing that the chain smoker, who can't survive for more than an hour without a cigarette, can go from sunrise to sunset during this month. There must be a psychological explanation for this. In this way, people are distanced from their bad habits and directed toward good, beneficial behavior. Ramadan carries much more importance than is generally thought.

THE INFLUENCE OF RAMADAN ON THE INDIVIDUAL AND ON SOCIETY

Ramadan has a great influence on both the individual and on society. When we look at it from the point of view of the individual, we can see that the individual undergoes a spiritual check-up during this month. Reflecting on creation, the mystery and true meaning of being human strengthens one's belief, helps to develop positive emotions, and prevents one from falling into the pitfalls of bad habits. This happens for the simple reason that it is not only the stomach that is fasting; a Muslim's hands, feet, ears, and mind all fast as well. The tongue refrains from gossip, from telling lies, from slander, from interfering in the relationships of others and back-stabbing, the hands refrain from that which is *haram* (forbidden) according to religion, the feet refrain from approaching any *haram* deed, the ears refrain from listening to any *haram* word, the mind and the heart refrain from any sedition or mischief. In this way, the individual develops in a positive way.

Moreover, the individual remains hungry from dawn until dusk. This is a training of willpower; that is the willpower is strengthened, and the one who is fasting gains in self-confidence and self-control.

After this brief glance at the effect of Ramadan on the individual, it is much easier to understand the effect of Ramadan on society as a whole. In brief, we can say the following.

Ramadan puts society through a spiritual sieve. People feel happier and more at peace during this month. The family members gather to eat the predawn meal; they share time together and share their thoughts and troubles, bringing family cooperation to a higher level. Friends and relatives gather for the fast-breaking meal; the fact that the rich gather with the poor, that the young and the old come together with small children strengthens solidarity within society. Ramadan is of extraordinary importance from the point of view of its reflections on society, in particular the fact that in the complicated business life of this modern age, there is a meal with meaning and value that brings people together, of their own free will, with absolutely no compulsion, to share the meaning, value and atmosphere of Ramadan.

Statistics show that the crime rate falls off during Ramadan. This is another example of the positive influence of Ramadan on society as a whole.

THE PURPOSE OF FASTING FOR ONE MONTH OUT OF TWELVE

It would be useful to give the following information before examining the purpose of fasting for one month of the year. In Islam, worship is performed for God. The most esteemed worship is that which is done, *"Because God ordered it thus and that which is only for Him."*

If one takes this into account when considering the mystery and wisdom of worship, then the reason and fine points that lay behind fasting for one month can easily be understood.

Fasting comes at the head of the forms of worship that are performed to attain the pleasure of God and to attain His approval. As a matter of fact, according to Prophet Muhammad, Muslims should only fast for God, and hypocrisy should have no place in worship. Therefore, the blessings involved in fasting are so great that they cannot be measured. Muslims who fast develop feelings of tenderness and mercy. They experience what the hungry and poor live with every day. They learn to put up with hunger and thirst through their fast, and they develop patience and perseverance. Doctors have already made clear the benefits of fasting for the body; fasting provides the body's organs with an opportunity to rest, and this has been stated as being very beneficial. That is, fasting helps people attain physical and spiritual health. It provides us with an opportunity for self-control (for an examination of the carnal self). One of the most difficult tasks for a human being is to examine their inner selves and, being critical of their errors, to resolve on improvement. In our opinion, one of the most important purposes of Ramadan is that it helps a person toward determination and resolution.

Fasting in Ramadan encompasses all of the physical and spiritual being; it is a source of soundness, health, happiness, peace, and joy.

THE NIGHT OF POWER (LAYLAT AL-QADR)

The Night of Power is the year's most virtuous night. The Qur'an first began to be revealed to the Prophet on this night. The Qur'an is an eternal blessing given to the Prophet by God. The chapter of Qadr in the Qur'an is concerned about this night:

> Behold, We have sent it (the Qur'an) down in the Night of Power. What is it that enables you to perceive what the Night of Power is? The Night of Power is better than a thousand months. The angels and the Spirit descend throughout it by the permission of their Lord with His decrees for every affair; (it is) pure mercy and security from all misfortunes (for the servants who spend it in devotion in appreciation of its worth). It lasts until the rise of the dawn.[41]

For a long time, the Night of Qadr, which Prophet Muhammad told the Companions to search for after the twentieth day of Ramadan, has long been accepted as falling on the 27th night of the month.

Let's take a look at some of the things that the Prophet said concerning this night:

> "Some of you have seen in your dreams that the Night of Power falls in the first seven (days). Others have seen that it is in the last seven (days). Look for it in the last ten (days)."[42]

> "...Look for it in the last ten odd-numbered nights."[43]

The report that most fully discusses this matter is that of the Companion Abu Said al-Hudri. He reported that the Prophet said the following:

"I secluded myself away to search for the Night of Power in the first ten days. I continued my seclusion on the next ten days. Then an angel came and told me the Night of Power was in the last ten days,"

The Prophet then went on to say,

"Those who wish to go into seclusion with me should do so in the last ten days."

Those people secluded themselves with the Prophet. The Prophet then said,

"The Night of Power was shown to me as being one night."[44]

As we can see, the Prophet himself said that the Night of Power is to be found in the last ten days of Ramadan, and there is strong evidence that it consists of only one night. The fact that the Prophet would increase his worship more in the last ten days, that he would direct his family members to do the same, and that he would seclude himself during the last ten days, are all indicators of this as well.

According to information in Islamic sources, not only is the Night of Power hidden, the exact time of the following are hidden as well:

- The time on Friday when prayers are accepted
- The middle prayer or the perfect prayer (*salat al-wusta*— see Baqara 2:238) among the five daily prayers
- The Greatest Name of God (*Ism al-Azam*)
- The approval of God within all the prayers and worship
- The Day of Judgment in time
- Death in life

The aim behind these things being hidden is to keep Muslims perpetually in a state of full awareness of their obligations in front of God.

The word "Qadr" has been defined in three different ways by Islamic scholars:

1. *Night of Judgment*: The night when divine judgments are sorted.
2. *Honor and grandeur*
3. *Night of Pressure*: The Night of Power has been seen to be a night in which the Earth is pressed down upon by descending angels. "Pressure" has been interpreted to indicate the many future great blessings that will occur in its aftermath; the first revelation came after Gabriel squeezed the Prophet, leaving him breathless.[45]

MORE BLESSED THAN A THOUSAND MONTHS

The Night of Power is better than a thousand months . . . This good news from sura Qadr of the Qur'an is strong and distinct enough to require no further comment. Therefore, it is the brightest and strongest evidence of the lofty blessings of the Night of Power.

It is important to look and understand this night from the point of view of the following report about the Prophet.

First the Prophet was shown how long human life had lasted before his time. When he saw this, he found the lifetime of his nation to be very brief. He thought that as his community's life was so short in comparison to others, they would not have time to carry out the same good deeds as those who had had a longer life. This is why God granted him the Night of Power, which is more blessed than a thousand months.[46]

MAKING USE OF THIS NIGHT

The Prophet told us:

> "The person who sincerely believes in the blessings of the Night of Power and prays during the night will be forgiven their past sins."[47]

There are a few things that Muslims should do on this holy night, if they wish to pass it in an appropriate manner:

1. They should pray, worship and develop their feeling of servanthood in order to please God on this night.

2. They should read the Qur'an, listen to those who read it, think about the meaning, and refresh feelings of love and commitment to it.

3. They should invoke peace and blessings on Prophet Muhammad, have hope in his intercession, be conscious of themselves as a member of his community, and refresh their devotion to him.

4. They should listen to sermons and discussions in order to disperse the fog induced in their heart by the troubles and strife of daily life.

5. They should participate in discussions that have been prepared by those who have expertise in religious matters concerning the importance of this night. Such talks allow them to listen to themselves, to take account of their own personal inner world, to underline their errors, to eliminate deficiencies, and moreover act as a means for strengthening solidarity, friendship, conversation, unity, and togetherness.

6. They should repent and offer penitence, and undergo a serious examination of their carnal self. They should resolve not to repeat the same errors, and endeavor to steer themselves in a more beneficial direction.

7. They should engage in remembering God and contemplate on creation. Hearts that remember God find security. Those who contemplate the infinite power of Almighty God in the universe are able to strengthen belief in their hearts.

8. They should pray frequently. Prayer is the loftiest means of bringing a servant closer to God. It is reported that the Prophet prayed the following prayer much on this night: "God! You are the forgiver, you love to forgive; forgive me as well!"

9. It is very blessed to treat the day of the Night of Power in the same manner as the night itself. If this is done, then the spiritual light will be felt very deeply in the hearts of Muslims.

10. As a means of paying respect to this night, a Muslim should wish for God to forgive all Muslims. The Night of Power should act as a means to strengthen the bonds of brotherhood and love, it should bring together the world of Islam, and Muslims should desire that all people be kept safe from harm and trouble.

THE FESTIVAL OF RAMADAN (EID AL-FITR)

A t the time when Prophet Muhammad honored Madina with his presence, there were two Eids being celebrated there. On those days, there were games and celebrations. The Prophet, who witnessed these, said:

> "Almighty God has allotted the *Eid al-Fitr* (the Festival of Ramadan) and *Eid al-Adha* (the Festival of Sacrifice) as more blessed than these two festivals."[48]

Thus, from the Age of Happiness on, the Islamic world has celebrated two religious festivals.

Muslims receive a great blessing by being able to sense a shared spiritual air on the tranquil Eid morning.

DAYS OF FORGIVENESS AND REWARD

By the end of Ramadan, for one month, Muslims have risen from their beds very early for the predawn meal; they have opened their hands to plead, to implore, to repent, to beg forgiveness from Almighty God at daybreak; and they have prayed and asked for mercy. They have endured a variety of hardships during the day, remaining without food or water, and showing patience and endurance. They have endured their fast with not only a physical, but also a spiritual asceticism—that is, they have controlled their stomachs, their tongues and their hearts, so they have success-fully passed this test of servanthood. They have broken their fast with the evening call to prayer; they have climbed toward a joy of the spirit and the soul; they have fed the poor, the orphaned, the lonely, the stranger and they have shared their table with friends and relatives... They have gone to the *tarawih*: they have placed their heads to the ground in a joyful congregation; they have prayed together; vengeance, ambition, enmity have all been eliminated, one by one; and they have become humble, mature, sincere servants of God.

Thus, it is with these earnest efforts that the days have rolled up toward the day of the Eid; the Eid has arrived and today they will attain Divine forgiveness. Today their faces will smile, their hearts will be full of joy, and their houses will become places of celebration.

DAYS OF BROTHERHOOD-UNITY-SOLIDARITY

Eid days are days when the feelings of brother and sisterhood are most apparent. Those who have fallen out make up and friends are reunited, while everyone, adult and child, does what is required of them. Relatives and neighbors visit one another, respect is paid to elders, everybody's health and general situation are enquired about, elders are visited and efforts are made to bring together those who have fallen out in the neighborhood—as everyone supports such efforts. On this day, the children put on their best clothes; and orphans, the poor and those without homes are not forgotten. We should never forget, when the thorn was pulled from the foot of the orphan that Almighty God let roses blossom in its place and blessed the charitable soul who performed the action with happiness in his grave.

In a word, any act of charity, goodness or help will never go unanswered.

THE EID PRAYER

In many Muslim societies people get up early on Eid. If possible, they have a bath; if this is not possible, then they make *wudu* and put on clean garments. They walk to the mosque in an unhurried, sedate manner, remembering God and glorifying His Name. On Ramadan Eid, it is the tradition of the Prophet to eat something sweet before leaving the house for the Eid prayer, but on the Eid of Sacrifice, it is best if the first thing to be eaten is from the sacrificed animal. (But, nowadays in big cities the sacrificing of an animal does not happen quickly; therefore, this may not be possible.) In the same way, the young, the old, even children all go to the mosque together, or follow one another in quick succession; this helps the younger generations, in particular, desire to participate in the prayer.

Muslims attend the Eid prayers in great masses; this prayer only occurs twice a year and it is observed as a congregation. Therefore, it is likely that the Eid prayer could be the first occasion for many Muslims to come to the mosque.

After the Eid prayer has been prayed and the sermon has been listened to, the people pour out of the mosque and congratulate one another on the Eid, either in the garden of the mosque, or in their neighborhood, or in the local halls, according to the custom of the place.

FASTING IN SHAWWAL

According to the Islamic calendar, the month of Shawwal follows the month of Ramadan. Prophet Muhammad related that it was blessed to fast for six days in the month of Shawwal after the Ramadan Eid. The hadith that reports this is as follows:

> "For whoever fasts during Ramadan and then fasts for six days during Shawwal it will be as if they have fasted for the entire year."[49]

As we can see from the joyful news given to us in this hadith, anyone who fasts for six days during Shawwal after having fasted during Ramadan shall be considered as having fasted for an entire year. One explanation regarding this hadith could be that every good deed is rewarded ten times as much. When one multiples the thirty days of Ramadan and six days from Shawwal by ten we arrive at approximately the number of days in one year.

PILGRIMAGE IN DHU AL-HIJJA

D hu al-Hijja is the time for the Hajj, the major pilgrimage. The *tashrik* days (see Takbir below) and the Eid of the Sacrifice also fall in the month of Dhu al-Hijja. These, and the worship practiced on these days, are an important event among Muslims.

A hadith has come down to us concerning this month, reported by Ibn al-Abbas. In this hadith the Prophet tells us the following:

> "The worship performed during the month of Dhu al-Hijja is loved more by God than those good and beneficial deeds performed throughout the rest of the year."[50]

PILGRIMAGE

The Hajj, or the major pilgrimage, is one of the five pillars of Islam. It consists of visiting the holy precincts in Makka during the month of Dhu al-Hijja. The hajj is a rehearsal of life in both this world and the next, a theater of all Islamic life based upon deep devotion to God and the perception of one's servanthood and God's Divinity and Lordship. It consists of love, action, humility, God-consciousness, sacrifice, and dominion over the carnal self.

It has two pillars: staying at the plain of Arafat near Makka for a certain length of time on the ninth of Dhu al-Hijja, and circumambulating the Ka'ba any day after staying at Arafat. *Ihram* is also essential to both the major (Hajj) and minor pilgrimage (*Umra*). *Ihram* is the intention to perform either Hajj or Umra, or both, and marks the beginning of Hajj or Umra, or both if they are performed together. It also signifies that some things have become forbidden. Men wear special attire while in *ihram*—two white, unstitched sheets; this attire itself is called *ihram* by some. As stated above, if we take into consideration that the pilgrimage falls on the first ten days of the month of Dhu al-Hijja, then we can more easily understand why the blessings derived from the forms of worship practiced during this time are esteemed as being blessed and virtuous. These days, with the prayers of the millions of pilgrims who are now able to complete this form of worship, are very productive, very blessed. Pilgrims chant *talbiya* (see below), glorify God's name, cry out His Unity and existence, and invoke peace and blessings on the Prophet. Some of the prayers chanted by pilgrims are below:

Talbiya

Labbayk Allahumma labbayk, labbayka la sharika laka labbayk, Inna'l-Hamda wa'n-ni'mata laka wa'l-mulk, la sharika lak:

Dear God! I accept your invitation. I bow my head before your commands. I relinquish to you all that I own. You have no partner. I accept your invitation, over and over again. Without a doubt, all thanks are due to you. You have no partner.

Takbir

Allahu Akbar Allahu Akbar, la ilaha illallahu wallahu Akbar, Allahu Akbar wa lillahi'l-Hamd

God is the greatest. God is the greatest. There is no god but God. God is the greatest. God is the greatest. All thanks are due to God.

Tahlil

La ilaha illallahu wahdahu la sharika lah. Lahu'l-Mulku walahu'l-Hamdu ve huwa ala kulli shay'in qadir

There is no god but God. He is One. All property belongs to Him. His power is sufficient for everything.

Salawat al-Sharif

Allahumma salli ala sayyidina Muhammadin wa ala al-i sayyidina Muhammad. Kama sallayta ala sayyidina Ibrahima wa ala al-i sayyidina Ibrahim. Wabarik ala sayyidina Muhammadin wa ala

*al-i sayyidina Muhamammad. Kama barakta ala seyyidina Ibrahima
wa ala al-i sayyidina Ibrahima fi'l-alamin. Innaka Hamidun Majid.*

O God, let your mercy come upon Muhammad and the family of
Muhammad as you sent mercy to Abraham and his family. Give
many blessings to Muhammad and the family of Muhammad, as
you have given many blessings to Abraham and his family in the
worlds. Truly You are the Praiseworthy and Glorious.

The pilgrims, with prayers on their lips and their hearts filled
with light, go to Arafat on the day before the Eid to pray and
stay there. They go on to stay in Muzdalifa (the holy place between
Arafat and Mina), continuing to throw pebbles at the Jamarat,
the rocks that symbolize one's carnal self in Mina, sacrifice an
animal, and circumambulate the Ka'ba (For further information
on the Hajj and its rituals, see Büyükçelebi, *Living in the Shade
of Islam*, The Light Publishing).

For all believers who reach the month of Dhu al-Hijja, wherever they may be, their hearts are with the pilgrims who are in
those holy places; in their prayers, they say, "O God, please include
this prayer in those that are being made in Masjid al-Haram, in
Baytullah (the Ka'ba), in the Masjid al-Nabi, in the Masjid al-
Quba,li" and become one with the pilgrims. At the same time, all
the pilgrims are praying for their brethren who have not been
able to come to the holy places; in other words, believers all over
the world are partners in prayer.

Moreover, at the end of the twenty-three obligatory (*fard*)
prayers that take place from the morning of the eve of the Eid
to the afternoon prayer of the fourth day, it is necessary to say
tashrik takbir. The meaning of the *tashrik takbir* is the same as the
takbir above; *"Allahu Akbar Allahu Akbar. La ilaha illallahu wallahu Akbar. Allahu Akbar walillahi'l hamd."*

THE FESTIVAL OF SACRIFICE (EID AL-ADHA)

In commemoration of the willingness of Prophet Abraham to obey God's command to sacrifice his son, Ishmael, Muslims celebrate Eid al-Adha every year; this Eid falls on the tenth day of Dhu al-Hijja and lasts for four days. Pleased with Abraham's submission, God put a ram in the place of Ishmael to be sacrificed instead. It has become the tradition since that time to sacrifice an animal. Traditionally, Muslims follow the footsteps of Prophet Abraham and they share one third of the meat with the poor, one third with their neighbors and relatives, and keep the final third for the use of their of own family.

There are only specific animals that can be sacrificed and they can only be sacrificed within a specific time, if this action is to be considered as a form of worship. It has been stated that, "sheep, goats, cattle, and camels are seen as being religiously permissible." The time period when this action is permissible consists of the days of the Festival of Sacrifice.

According to Imam Azam, it is obligatory for Muslims to sacrifice an animal at this time. The verse in the Qur'an *So pray and sacrifice (an animal) for God,*[52] is evidence of this.

Islamic scholars have indicated some hadiths to prove the obligatory nature of the sacrifice. The Prophet ordered:

> "Sacrifice an animal. It is the tradition of your forefather Abraham."[53]

> "Let no one approach a place of worship (mosque or masjid) who has not made a sacrifice if they are of those who are in a suitable situation (with wealth according to the set religious standards)"[54]

WHO SACRIFICES AN ANIMAL?

Those who are free, not traveling, Muslim, and have wealth according to the set religious standards (who own enough property to have to pay the annual alms) are those who must perform this duty.

Some scholars also state that being mature and of a sound mind are also preconditions for sacrificing an animal, and according to Imam Azam and Imam Abu Yusuf, those who find themselves as guardians of those who do not fulfill these two conditions should sacrifice an animal in their name.

The standards measuring whether or not one should sacrifice an animal are the same as those that measure whether or not one should pay the *sadaqa al-fitr.* Like that of *zakat,* the wealth that constitutes the obligation to sacrifice an animal is based on trade goods or money earned; there is no condition that the amount have been possessed for a year or that it should have growth-potential. For this reason, those who were poor, but have suddenly come into money on the Eid days must sacrifice an animal. Those who were wealthy, but have suddenly fallen on bad times are not required to do so.

ANIMALS OF SACRIFICE

The animals that are suitable for sacrifice are sheep and goats (which are a year old, or seven to eight months, which is considered the same as having fulfilled one year of life), cattle (two years of age or more), oxen (two years of age or more), and camels (five years of age or more).

A sheep or a goat can only be sacrificed in the name of one person. A camel or cow can be shared from between one to seven people. However, the partners must all be Muslim, they must all purchase equal shares of the animal, and they must sacrifice the animal in the name of God.

An animal cannot be sacrificed if one or both eyes are blind, if most of the teeth have fallen out, if the ears have been cut, if one or both horns have been broken off from the base, if more than half an ear or the tail is missing, if it was born without ears or a tail, if the bones are so thin that they do not contain any marrow, if the animal is too lame to walk to the place where it will be sacrificed, or if it is ill.

If the animal is cross-eyed, if it is lame (but can walk), if it was born with horns, or without horns, if the horns are slightly damaged, if the ear has a hole in it, or is torn breadthways, if the tips of the ears have been cut or they hang down, if some of the teeth are missing, or are twisted, then there is nothing to prevent the animal from being sacrificed.

The Prophet said: "Eat from the sacrifice, donate it and collect it."[55] From this hadith, we can understand that a Muslim should offer some of the meat to guests, donate some to the needy, and give the rest to the members of their family.

The person who sacrifices an animal can donate the hide to a charity, use it in their house as a prayer mat, or sell it, giving the money to a charity. The person who has sacrificed an animal cannot sell the hide and spend the money themselves.

It is traditional for the person who has sacrificed the animal to pray two units (*rakats*) to thank Almighty God, to pray to Him, and to plead with God to accept the sacrifice.

THE GLAD TIDINGS OF THE PROPHET

If a Muslim sacrifices an animal in sincerity, he or she will see the return multiplied on the Day of Judgment. The Prophet said the following on this matter:

> "There is no more beloved action than that of a person sacrificing an animal on the Day of Sacrifice for God. That sacrifice will come with its horns, hide and hooves."[56]

THE PURPOSE OF THE SACRIFICE

Alongside those members of society who are wealthy or well-off are those who go for months without seeing meat, who wander around half-full, people with honor who do not make their position clear for all to see, people who live in hidden poverty. These people often refrain from asking for anything from anyone. It is for such people that the feast after the sacrifice has been established. It brightens their hearts and allows them a share in the welfare of society. The feast of the sacrifice helps to spread social justice and strengthens the ties of love.

The above factors have beneficial effects from a social and economic view, in that they help the individual toward peace and happiness, and they help them to gain maturity. Sacrifice—through thanks, gratitude, forbearance, and sharing—nurtures both the individual and the society.

THE MONTH OF MUHARRAM

The month of Muharram is one of the holy months in which warfare has been traditionally forbidden; this was so even before the advent of Islam. The other months are Dhu al-Qada, Dhu al-Hijja, and Rajab. There are some hadiths concerning the month of Muharram. The Prophet told us that:

> "The most blessed month in which to fast, other than Ramadan, is the holy month of Muharram (which is honored as The Month of God)."[57]

Ashura has been a day of fasting for Muslims since the early Muslim community. According to Abdullah ibn Abbas, when Prophet Muhammad came to Madina, he saw the Jews fasting on the tenth of Muharram in celebration of the prophet Moses' victory over the Pharaoh. Upon this, the Prophet fasted on Ashura day and ordered others to fast as well.[58]

According to other narrations, the Prophet recommended that the Companions fast on the day of Ashura before the compulsory Ramadan fast; in fact, according to the above hadith, he actually demanded that they do so. But after fasting Ramadan became obligatory he said the following:

> "It is without a doubt that the Day of Ashura is one of God's days. From now on, who so wishes should fast on that day; who so wishes does not have to." In this way, fasting on this day was left up to individual choice.[59]

In another hadith one of the companions was told that he should "fast three days in the months of Rajab, Dhu al-Qada, Dhu al-Hijja, and Muharram."[60] Another hadith states that these three days in the final month should be "the day before Ashura, the day of Ashura, and the following day."

The day of Ashura falls on the tenth day of the month of Muharram. The word "*ashura*" actually means the "tenth day." Moreover, there are opinions that state "Almighty God granted ten gifts to ten prophets on that day. Or because God granted blessings to the community of Muhammad on this day, it is known as Ashura."

The month in which Ashura falls is generally known as the month of Ashura. Although there are various reports concerning what actually lies behind the day of Ashura, the fact that the ninth, tenth, and eleventh days of this month (Muharram) have been considered as holy, blessed days is an important point that must be taken into consideration.

NOAH AND THE FLOOD

One of the most important pieces of popular knowledge surrounding the events of the day of Ashura in the Islamic world is its connection with the flood and Noah. The flood occurred on that day, and it is said that the ark rested on Mount Judi,[61] reaching safety, on that day. Again, according to popular knowledge, Noah fasted on this day to show his thanks and gratitude to God.

Prophet Noah was sent to people by God because they had begun to deviate from the truth after Prophet Adam and Prophet Enoch. Prophet Noah explained to people the belief in one God, and invited them to the way of truth, forbidding them from worshipping idols.

But they were bereft of the lofty soul necessary to understand the announcement and invitation of Noah that would be necessary to discover beauty. Prophet Noah found himself the prophet to these unruly people. According to the Qur'an, he told them

> Surely I am a plain warner for you. That you shall not serve any but God, surely I fear for you the punishment of a painful day. (Shuara 26:106-110; Hud 11:25-26)

THE ANSWER OF THE UNRULY

These people, who were unruly and denied the truth, made fun of Prophet Noah's holy call:

> We do not consider you but a mortal like ourselves, and we do not see any have followed you but those who are the meanest of us at first thought and we do not see in you any excellence over us; nay, we deem you liars. (Hud 11:27)

They perceived those poor people who followed Noah and his call, who believed in God as a loving servant, as being contemptible; they said they would not be found under the same roof as them and that they were greater. They could not understand that superiority lay not in money, goods, or property, but in the worship of one God, good morals, and behavior that is beneficial to society.

However, those people who they saw as despicable were people who were worth many times their value in the eyes of God. Therefore, Prophet Noah would not desert the side of these poor, worthy people; he could not turn his back on them merely because the unruly people said he should do so. As a matter of fact, he displayed forbearance and patience on this path.

Unfortunately, none of the leaders of the tribe showed any understanding of Noah, even though he did not expect any material benefit. All he wanted was for them to believe in God. But this just was not possible. When he told them what they should believe, they went so far as to label him mad; and in order to keep him under control, they kept him under surveillance.

When Prophet Noah refused to be turned from his way, despite all the problems he had been caused, they decided to threaten him with death. Prophet Noah met this threat with patience and forbearance, declaring the unity of God and belief in His way. But the eyes that saw the way to truth, the ears that heard the truth, the hearts that spoke His name, and those with the courage to defend righteousness, were few. Finally, Prophet Noah begged God:

> "O my Lord! Truly my people have rejected me. Judge Thou, then, between me and them openly, and deliver me and those of the Believers who are with me." (Shuara 26:117-118)

Almighty God accepted Noah's prayer and taught him first of all how to make the Ark. In this way, the believers started to build the Ark under the supervision of Prophet Noah. As the building progressed, those who had lost their way made fun of Prophet Noah and the believers who were with him. Prophet Noah reminded them that there would come a day when those who were making fun of them would no longer exist. But there was no sign that those who denied the truth had yet awoken. They said: "Alright, then. Let the torment about which you speak so much come and we will see." And they continued to make fun of the believers.

THE FLOOD STARTS

Almighty God ordered that the believers board the Ark with a pair of every animal. The heavenly doors opened and water poured down. Water poured out of the Earth as well. The two sources of water combined. The wife of Prophet Noah and one of his sons were among the unbelievers. He had warned them many times of what was to come. But they thought that if such a disaster were to come, that they would be able to save themselves by climbing to the peaks of the mountains, and so they refused to contemplate that what Noah was saying could be true. While the believers were safe in the Ark, the unbelievers drowned, one by one; the torment that had inflicted on him when they had made fun of him came and took them by the back of the necks, dragging them down in whirlpools.

Prophet Noah prayed that the Ark would land in a bountiful, calm place, and his prayers were answered; he was of those whose prayers are answered. Almighty God ordered:

> "O Earth! Swallow up your water, and O sky! Withold (your rain)!" (Hud 11:44)

Upon this order the thunder was stopped, the water streaming from the Earth ceased, and the Ark landed on Mount Judi. In this way were God's Prophet and the believers saved.

ASHURA PUDDING

According to reports, upon being saved from the flood, the believers opened their provisions and mixed together wheat kernels, garbanzo beans, and other dried goods, cooked them all together, with the resulting pudding being so bountiful that everyone was able to eat their fill.

Even though many thousands of years have passed since that day, believers make a pudding known as ashura on this day in memory of this event. It is traditional to make this pudding and offer it to one's family and friends, and to offer it to neighbors; this is something that has become extremely common nowadays. Every year in the month of Muharram people, be they in villages or cities, come together and celebrate the salvation of those who believed in Noah.

There are many traditions that bring the young and old together, uniting all the members of the community; this leads to solidarity and cooperation. The tradition of ashura, which seems to be merely the consumption of something sweet, is an important component that symbolizes spiritual values and which creates an atmosphere of kinship.

We have reported the historical events that lie behind the month of Muharram and the ashura pudding. But, in fact, there are many other historical events that occurred in the month of Muharram. To give some examples, Prophet Abraham was saved from the fire into which he was thrown, Prophet Job found relief from his debilitating illness, and Prophet Moses and his tribe passed through the Red Sea.

Among all these events, there is an event that occurred on 10 Muharram 61 (10 October 680) that is so clear that it throws believing hearts into grief, and causes tears to gush from the eyes.

On this date, the grandson of Prophet Muhammad, Husayn, was martyred by merciless bloodthirsty people in Karbala.

Muslims take a lesson from the salvation of the believers who followed Noah, but at the same time they pay tribute to the blessed souls of Husayn and other members of the Prophet's family who were murdered in this tragic event.

DATES OF THE BLESSED DAYS AND NIGHTS

T he Islamic Calendar is lunar-based and a lunar year is short-er than a solar year. Due to this difference, the blessed dates comes 10–12 days earlier every year. Thus, people around the world afforded an equal level of challenge and reward through their lifetimes (e.g. in Ramadan they fast sometimes through short winter days and sometimes in long summer days).

2005

Days and Nights	Muslim Calendar (Hijri - AH)		Common Era
	MONTH	YEAR	
	Dhu al-Hijja 1	1425	January 11
Festival of Sacrifice Eve	Dhu al-Hijja 9	1425	January 19
Festival of Sacrifice (Eid al-Adha)	Dhu al-Hijja 10	1425	January 20
Festival of Sacrifice (Eid al-Adha)	Dhu al-Hijja 11	1425	January 21
Festival of Sacrifice (Eid al-Adha)	Dhu al-Hijja 12	1425	January 22
Festival of Sacrifice (Eid al-Adha)	Dhu al-Hijja 13	1425	January 23
New Year (Hijri)	Muharram 1	1426	February 10
Ashura	Muharram 10	1426	February 19
	Safar 1	1426	March 11
	Rabi al-Awwal 1	1426	April 10
Mawlid	Rabi al-Awwal 11/12	1426	April 20/21
	Rabi al-Thani 1	1426	May 09
	Jumada Awwal 1	1426	June 08
	Jumada Thani 1	1426	July 08
Beginning of Blessed Three Months	Rajab 1	1426	August 06
Laylat al-Raghaib	Rajab 6/7	1426	August 11/12
Laylat al-Mi'raj	Rajab 26/27	1426	August / September 31/01
	Shaban 1	1426	September 05
Laylat al-Bara'a	Shaban 14/15	1426	September 18/19
	Ramadan 1	1426	October 05
Laylat al-Qadr (Night of Power)	Ramadan 26/27	1426	October 30/31
Festival of Ramadan Eve	Ramadan 29	1426	November 02
Festival of Ramadan (Eid al-Fitr)	Shawwal 1	1426	November 03
Festival of Ramadan (Eid al-Fitr)	Shawwal 2	1426	November 04
Festival of Ramadan (Eid al-Fitr)	Shawwal 3	1426	November 05
	Dhu al-Qada 1	1426	December 03

2006

Days and Nights	Muslim Calendar (Hijri - AH)		Common Era
	MONTH	YEAR	
	Dhu al-Hijja 1	1426	January 1
Festival of Sacrifice Eve	Dhu al-Hijja 9	1426	January 09
Festival of Sacrifice (Eid al-Adha)	Dhu al-Hijja 10	1426	January 10
Festival of Sacrifice (Eid al-Adha)	Dhu al-Hijja 11	1426	January 11
Festival of Sacrifice (Eid al-Adha)	Dhu al-Hijja 12	1426	January 12
Festival of Sacrifice (Eid al-Adha)	Dhu al-Hijja 13	1426	January 13
New Year (Hijri)	Muharram 1	1427	January 31
Ashura	Muharram 10	1427	February 09
	Safar 1	1427	March 1
	Rabi al-Awwal 1	1427	March 30
Mawlid	Rabi al-Awwal 11/12	1427	April 09/10
	Rabi al-Thani 1	1427	April 29
	Jumada Awwal 1	1427	May 28
	Jumada Thani 1	1427	June 27
Beginning of Blessed Three Months	Rajab 1	1427	July 26
Laylat al-Raghaib	Rajab 6/7	1427	July 27/28
Laylat al-Mi'raj	Rajab 26/27	1427	August 20/21
	Shaban 1	1427	August 25
Laylat al-Bara'a	Shaban 14/15	1427	September 07/08
	Ramadan 1	1427	September 24
Laylat al-Qadr (Night of Power)	Ramadan 26/27	1427	October 19/20
Festival of Ramadan Eve	Ramadan 29	1427	October 22
Festival of Ramadan (Eid al-Fitr)	Shawwal 1	1427	October 23
Festival of Ramadan (Eid al-Fitr)	Shawwal 2	1427	October 24
Festival of Ramadan (Eid al-Fitr)	Shawwal 3	1427	October 25
	Dhu al-Qada 1	1427	November 22
	Dhu al-Hijja 1	1427	December 22
Festival of Sacrifice Eve	Dhu al-Hijja 9	1427	December 30
Festival of Sacrifice (Eid al-Adha)	Dhu al-Hijja 10	1427	December 31
Festival of Sacrifice (Eid al-Adha)	Dhu al-Hijja 11	1427	January 01, 2007
Festival of Sacrifice (Eid al-Adha)	Dhu al-Hijja 12	1427	January 02, 2007
Festival of Sacrifice (Eid al-Adha)	Dhu al-Hijja 13	1427	January 03, 2007

ABOUT THE AUTHOR

Hüseyin Algül was born in 1945 in Konya, Turkey. He graduated from Istanbul Higher Institute of Islam in 1968. After working as a teacher of religion in secondary schools for a few years, he went on his academic career starting at Bursa Higher Institute of Islam in 1975. He obtained his Ph.D. degree on Islamic history at Uludağ University Faculty of Theology. He became full professor in 1996 at the same faculty, where he continues teaching Islam.

BIBLIOGRAPHY

Algül, Hüseyin, *İslam Tarihi* (History of Islam), I-III, Istanbul: 1986.

Algül, Hüseyin, *Peygamberimizin Şemaili, Ahlak ve Adabı* (The Prophet's Physical Description, Morality, and Manners), Nil yayınları, Izmir: 1989.

Ali al-Qari, *Sharh al-Shifa* (Interpretation of Healing), Istanbul AH 1308 (1891).

Beyatlı, Yahya Kemal, *Aziz Istanbul* (Istanbul, Beloved), Istanbul: 1985.

Bilmen, Ö. Nasuhi, *Büyük İslam İlmihali* (The Grand Book of Islamic Principles), Istanbul: 1958.

Bukhari, *al-Jami al-Sahih*, Istanbul, AH 1315 (1897).

Davudoğlu, Ahmet, *Interpretation of Bulugh al-Maram*, Istanbul.

Yazır, Elmalılı Hamdi, *Hak Dini Kur'an Dili* (Language of the Qur'an, the Divine Religion), Istanbul: 1979.

Sheikh Mansur Ali Nasif, *Tac Tercemesi* (The Translation of *Taj*). Translated into Turkish by Bekir Sadak. Istanbul: 1974.

Halabi, *Insan al-Uyun*, Beirut.

Husameddin Naqshbandi, *Sharh al-Shamail al-Nabi*, Egypt: AH 1254 (1838).

Ibn al-Athir, *al-Kamil*, Beirut: AH 1385 (1965).

Ibn Hisham, *al-Sirat al-Nabawiya*, Egypt: AH 1355 (1936).

Ibn Maja, *Sunan*, Egypt: AH 1373 (1954).

Ibn Sa'd, *Tabaqat*, Beirut.

ISAM (Islamic Research Center), *Ilmihal* (Book on Islamic Principles), Türkiye Diyanet Vakfı Publications, Istanbul: 1999.

Karaman, Hayreddin, *İslam'ın Işığında Günün Meseleleri* (Contemporary Matters under the Light of Islam), Istanbul: 1982.

Kılavuz, A. Saim, Akif Köten, Osman Çetin, Hüseyin Algül, *Kaynak Kitap* (The Reference Book), Marifet Yayınları, Istanbul: 1985.

Kazancı, Ahmed Lütfi, *Hz. Adem'den Hâtemü'l-Enbiyâ'ya Kur'ân'ın Tanıttığı Peygamberler* (The Prophets Mentioned in the Qur'an-from Adam to the Last of Messengers), Nil Yayınları, İzmir: 1990.

Köksal, M. Asım, *İslam Tarihi* (The History of Islam), Istanbul: 1981.

Kur'an-ı Kerim ve Türkçe Anlamı (The Holy Qur'an and Its Turkish Interpretation), DİB yayınları, Ankara: 1983.

Kur'an-ı Kerim ve Açıklamalı Meali (The Holy Qur'an and Its Translation with Annotation), DİV yayınları, Ankara 1993.

Kur'an-ı Hakim ve Meal-i Kerim (The Wise Qur'an and Its Translation). Translated and annotated by H. Basri Çantay, Istanbul: 1965.

M. Raif Efendi, *Muhtasar Şemail-i Şerif Tercemesi* (A Comprehensive Translation of the Blessed Physical Attributes of the Prophet), Istanbul: AH 1304 (1886).

Nevevi, *Riyadh al-Salihin*. Translated by K. Burslan, H. H. Erdem. Ankara: 1958-1964.

Sahih-i Buhari Muhtasarı Tecrid-i Sarih Tercemesi (A Comprehensive Translation of Sahih al-Bukhari, Tajrid al-Sarih). Translated by A. Naim, K. Miras. DİB Yayınları, Ankara: 1976.

Tirmizi, *Sunan*, Cairo: AH 1358 (1938).

NOTES

1   The names of the months in the Islamic calendar are: Muharram, Safar, Rabi al-Awwal, Rabi al-Thani, Jumada Awwal, Jumada Thani, Rajab, Shaban, Ramadan, Shawwal, Dhu al-Qada, Dhu al-Hijja.

2   For more information on *muhasaba* and other Sufi terms, see Gülen, *Key Concepts in the Practice of Sufism*, Vol.1, The Light, Inc., NJ: 2004, pp. 6-9)

3   Baqara 2:129

4   Tajrid, III, 3; Muslim, *Jum'a*, 19, 20

5   Bukhari (translation of *Tajrid al-Sarih*), III, 4-5; Muslim, *Jum'a*, 18

6   Muslim, *Jum'a*, 15

7   Muslim, *Jum'a*, 9

8   Muslim, *Jum'a*, 27

9   See, Muslim, *Siyam*, 148

10 Muslim, *Siyam*, 175

11 Muslim, *Siyam*, 177

12 Muslim, *Siyam*, 181

13 See, Muslim, *Siyam*, 181

14 Muslim, *Siyam*, 196

15 *Riyadh al-Salihin*, II, 512

16 *Riyadh al-Salihin*, II, 511

17 Muslim, *Siyam*, 202

18 See, *Riyadh al-Salihin*, II, 507

19 Muslim, *Siyam*, 175

20 Muslim, *Siyam*, 200

21 Najm 53:7-19

22 Concerning the Mi'raj the Noble Messenger said, "Salutations to God, eternity and dominion are His; all benedictions and supplications are to Him." Almighty God said that night, "Peace be upon you, O Prophet!" to which the Prophet replied the divine greeting, saying, "Peace be upon us and upon all God's righteous servants." Gabriel who took part in the conversation said that night at the divine command, "I testify that there

is no god but God, and I testify that Muhammad is God's Messenger. For more information about the *tashahhud*, see Nursi, *The Rays Collection*, The Sixth Ray, pp. 118-120; Büyükçelebi, *Living in the Shade of Islam*, NJ: 2005, p. 197.

23 Isra 17:1
24 Isra 17:22-29
25 See, Yazir, Elmalılı H., *Hak Dini Kur'an Dili*, VI, 4293-4297.
26 *al-Taj*, II, 154
27 See, Muslim, *Siyam*, 199-201
28 Muslim, *Siyam*,1
29 Muslim, *Siyam*, 2
30 Muslim, *Siyam*, 45; *Riyadh al-Salihin*, II, 495
31 Muslim, *Siyam*, 48
32 Muslim, *Siyam*, 49, 50
33 *Riyadh al-Salihin*, II, 517
34 See, *Riyadh al-Salihin*, II, 516
35 Muslim, *Salat al-Musafirun*, 173; *Riyadh al-Salihin*, II, 463
36 Muslim, *Salat al-Musafirun*, 173-174; *Riyadh al-Salihin*, II, 463
37 Muslim, *Siyam*, 163
38 Muslim, *Siyam*, 166
39 Muslim, *Fadail*, 50; *Riyadh al-Salihin*, II, 491
40 Muslim, *Itikaf*, 7
41 Qadr 97:1-5
42 Muslim, *Siyam*, 208
43 Muslim, *Siyam*, 212
44 Muslim, *Siyam*, 215
45 Yazır, Elmalılı Hamdi, *Hak Dini Kur'an Dili*, IX, 5969
46 *al-Taj*, II, 135
47 *Riyadh al-Salihin*, II, 464
48 *al-Taj*, I, 309
49 Muslim, *Si-yam*, 204
50 *Riyadhal-Salihin*, II, 507
51 Masjid al-Quba is the very first mosque built during the time of the Prophet, peace and blessings be upon him.
52 Kawthar 108:2
53 A. Davudoğlu, *Bülüğu'l-Meram Tercümesi ve Şerhi* (Translation and Interpretation of *Bulug al-Maram*), IV, 1
54 Ibn Maja, *Adahi*, 2
55 *al-Taj*, III, 217
56 *al-Taj*, III, 209

57 Muslim, *Siyam*, 202

58 Muslim, *Siyam*, 128

59 Muslim, *Siyam*, 117

60 *Riyadh al-Salihin*, II, 507

61 Judi: The mountain where the ark of Prophet Noah was landed according to the Qur'an (Hud 11:44): *Then the word went forth: "O Earth! Swallow up your water, and O sky! Withold (your rain)!" and the water abated, and the matter was ended. The Ark rested on (Mount) Judi, and the word went forth: "Away with those who do wrong!"* Mount Judi is located in south-east Turkey very close to Turkish-Iraqi border. With many caves, easy slopes, and certainly its hand-palm shaped top, its landscape looks suitable to accommodate after the flood. It is also reported that Judi might be the name of a mountain range across Mosul, Jizra and Damascus. Genesis 8:4 mentions Mount Ararat in eastern Turkey as the location where the ark landed.